What If?

Letters and Postcards from C&B

Robert and Cima Balser

ARCHWAY
PUBLISHING

Archway Publishing books may be ordered
through booksellers or by contacting:

Archway Publishing
1663 Liberty Drive
Bloomington, IN 47403
www.archwaypublishing.com
1 (888) 242-5904

Because of the dynamic nature of the Internet, any web addresses or
links contained in this book may have changed since publication and
may no longer be valid. The views expressed in this work are solely those
of the author and do not necessarily reflect the views of the publisher,
and the publisher hereby disclaims any responsibility for them.

Any people depicted in stock imagery provided by Thinkstock are
models, and such images are being used for illustrative purposes only.
Certain stock imagery © Thinkstock.

ISBN: 978-1-4808-5044-6 (sc)
ISBN: 978-1-4808-5043-9 (hc)
ISBN: 978-1-4808-5045-3 (e)

Library of Congress Control Number: 2017914597

Print information available on the last page.

Archway Publishing rev. date: 09/19/2017

"THE WORLD IS A BOOK AND

HE WHO STAYS HOME

READS ONLY ONE PAGE"

Anonymous

Bob's self portrait 1950

Dedication

TO BOB, OF COURSE, MY HUSBAND, LOVER, SOUL-MATE, BEST FRIEND, LIFE-LONG PARTNER, WHO WITH HIS FORMIDABLE TALENT, CREATIVITY, PROFESSIONALISM, BOUNDLESS ENERGY, ABILITY TO SOLVE PROBLEMS LARGE AND SMALL, COURAGE, CURIOSITY, HONESTY, GENEROSITY, KINDNESS, OVERFLOWING LOVE OF LIFE, AND NATURAL CHARM, MADE ALL OUR DREAMS COME TRUE.

Contents

Introduction

Over the years, whenever I've been asked where I'm from, I always start by explaining that my parents went to Europe in 1959, 12 years before I was born (in London), for what was supposed to be a six-month sabbatical, and were still there 40 years later. I explain that they did not fit the standard expatriate mold; they worked for neither a multinational corporation nor the Foreign Service. They were free spirits, made possible by my father's ability to produce animated film wherever there was an interesting opportunity, or whenever funds got low, allowing them to work, live, and travel in various European countries before finally settling in Barcelona, with his own animation studio, and where I grew up.

By the time I was born, my parents had already had enough adventures to fill a lifetime, but they weren't finished by a long shot. My childhood was filled with a constant stream of interesting, eccentric, creative people, smoke-filled art gallery openings, and film festivals in places like Zagreb, where I experienced the unique torture of Slavic animation.

I think what makes my parents' story so compelling is that they actually did what so many people only talk and dream about. But the key to their story, and something we can all learn from, was their uncommon ability to connect on a deep level with everyone they met, from a taxi driver to the queen of Denmark. My parents made friends easily, were good listeners, and were genuinely interested in your story. As a result they made life-long friends on almost every continent. My mother still exchanges Christmas cards with friends she hasn't seen in decades.

This story would also not be possible without my mother's keen powers of observation, humor, and disciplined chronicling of their daily life. She assiduously kept a diary to record their memorable experiences and the unique characters they met in their travels. It was these diaries she used to write the letters to family and friends that form the substance of this book.

So get ready to travel back in time as my mother paints a vivid picture of their adventures in 1959 Europe, such as blithely boarding a train to attend the Moscow Film Festival at the height of the Cold War.

Trevel Balser
February, 2017.

Preface

What if, on a Friday night in 1948, neither Bob nor I had gone to a campus club dance at UCLA? Each of us had had to be talked into going, I by a sometime boyfriend, and Bob by one of his best friends, would our paths ever have crossed again? He was an Art Major in his Junior year, and I, a Freshman English major. All I know is that when I went over to shake hands with this really cute blond, blue eyed guy I asked myself it this was the man with whom I was going to spend the rest of my life.

He must have thought that I was also kind of cute, because he pulled me right over to a short bench and we started to talk. Was he really an Art Major? (I was taking as many art history courses as I could), check. I was an English major. He recited pages of Kipling, check. We both laughed a lot, check, loved movies, check, and as he soon whirled me around the dance floor, turned out to be a great dancer, check. Added attraction: he had a Model A Ford and a ukulele to match, great fun, check. Last, but not least, I found out *on our very first date*, he was a great kisser, brazen to be sure, but check. On that first date, he said he didn't want to commit himself just yet but would like it if I didn't accept any other dates for the next six months. I hesitated what I thought was long enough to express my concern, and then just said, "O.K." but thought: "YES! YES! YES!"

What if, in Bob's senior year in UCLA's Art Department, the only class available which would fulfill the necessary requirements and credit he needed to graduate was "This dumb Animation Class" for which he had to return to campus the one night a week it was offered? We weren't yet married so any chance to be together a few more hours was most welcome, and I accompanied him and with permission, sat in on the class. We were enthralled. Taught by a Disney animator, Bill Shull, the first thing he said was that he wasn't going to teach "animation- you'll pick that up as you go. No, I'm going to teach you film making." And so he did, and excited as we both were, neither one of us could have possibly known or imagined how this "dumb class" would completely change and enrich our lives.

Bob and I continued to audit the class after he graduated – and we married – and as soon as he could, he began to free-lance at various animation studios in Hollywood. Eventually, in early 1959, with a few more What Ifs we left for Europe on what we hoped would be a six month sabbatical. The following pages, compiled from the letters and postcards I sent home, will give the reader some idea of how that first six month "sabbatical" was only the start of what lasted for forty adventure filled years. My hope is that you will enjoy reading about these first earliest days as much as Bob, now in Animation Heaven, and I had, living them.

Cima Balser
February, 2017

1

Plans

March 15, 1958

What if, sometime in 1958, most of the advertisement agencies in Los Angeles hadn't decided their viewers were tired of animated commercials and switched to live action, putting most free-lance animators out of work?

Would we have discovered we could actually live quite comfortably on my $85 salary? So that by the time the animation industry finally roared back into business again we were used to eating steak only two times a week instead of four or five, and decided to save Bob's $125, and maybe take a trip somewhere?

Next, What If, Mark, my hairdresser, hadn't just returned from his first trip to Europe so elated he could hardly restrain from pouring all his consumer research, along with shampoo on my head? I paid very close attention and followed his preliminary advice: Just put this new book, "Europe on $5 A Day" on the coffee table and let it lie there..."

Soon enough, Bob was asking, "Do you really think we

could do this on $5 a day?" My reply in all sincerity and big heart: "Sure, and if we camped, probably a lot less!"

FAST FORWARD: It has taken us almost a year to save enough for two one-way tickets on American Airlines to New York (stop over in Rochester to visit Bob's families), $99 each; two one-way tickets on the S.S Maasdam – Mark: "You must take the Maasdam, it's basically a one-class ship-oh, there's a small first class, but they're so bored they come down to our part of the ship." $200 each.

Having decided we aren't backpacker-hitchhiker types, nor bikers (what if it rains?) we also have a Peugeot 403 (seats fold back for camping overnights) paid for, to be picked up in Paris ($1,750 plus $200 shipping charge Europe-Los Angeles), and approximately $1,850 in travelers' checks, which, if "Europe On $5 A Day" is correct, we hope to make last for six months, if not completely carefree, semi-adventurous travel.

The Oldsmobile, refrigerator, stove, sofa, rugs, tables and chairs, and most of our other belongings have been sold or given away, leaving only three vanloads of our can't-part-withs, such as books, paintings, and rocks, put into storage (does everyone accumulate this much in nine years of marriage?).

We leave Los Angeles on April Fool's day, no comment.

Re: the photo-there simply was no room to pack Mom's old mink coat, which I certainly didn't need here, but if I'm lucky it will be snowing in Rochester.

Full up with anticipation,
C & B

Bob & Cima at Airport

2

Departure

April 1ˢᵗ, 1959

I hate these free post-cards they give you on planes. I get wrist-cramp trying to control a ball-point pen in mid-air. But give up a free postcard? Especially those that begin with "In Flight"....?

Well, what an April Fool's Day this has been. Our plane out of Los Angeles was delayed an hour, and I felt sorry for myself, burdened down as I was with three coats, (mom's five-pound mink was the top layer, for that casual look), and all my "hand luggage" (whose hands? how many? Even Shiva, the Indian goddess, wouldn't have been able to manage), and it was a balmy 98 on the airport thermometer.

Very rough flight this, can hardly eat my pot roast, not because I'm not well, but we seem to hit a downdraft every few minutes and the fork keeps slipping past my mouth and grazing my nose or cheek.

Hungrily,
C & B

April 1, 9 PM, Local Time, In Flight, Chicago-Rochester

Another free postcard. Missed our connections in Chicago due to the original delay this morning. We were bussed across Chicago to the other airport where we were treated to cocktails and dinner, but my fork kept hitting my cheek, I guess I was still compensating for those up and down-drafts. When they finally called our flight, it took so long to gather up all my coats and "hand luggage" again, we had to run. But all those bags were now in such disorder they kept slipping away, making me stop to pick them up again and again, and each time they became even more unwieldy, and we almost missed the plane.

Now they tell us they won't be able to take us all the way to Rochester. The crew will have been flying too long by then. They promised a limousine to drive us the 90 miles to Rochester, but when we arrived at the Buffalo airport at 3 am, (it certainly *had been* a memorable April Fools Day), there was no one in sight except for a few cleaning ladies. But Bob finally, somehow, managed to find someone with a car who could/would drive us there, "Toute suite." (Our French Phrase Book has gone to his head, or maybe so much time has passed since we left Los Angeles he thinks he's already in France.) The highway was deserted, there was a full moon, snow still on the ground, and I had those three coats to cuddle up to.

Dazed,
C & B

It was hard for us to catch up on our sleep in Rochester and visit with the family because grandma insisted we get three regular meals a day plus obligatory snacks. "Don't talk. Eat."

Not hungrily,
C & B

3

Enroute

April 20th In Sail.....

Well, did you ever think we'd make it on board? We checked to make sure the Railway Express box we sent directly to the ship containing my trusty Smith Corona not-really-so portable typewriter, air-mats, double sleeping bags, and a few extra winter clothes which we could very well have used last week in New York, did arrive and was held in the ship's hold.

It was snowing in New York – in April? So when we visited Aunt Paula and Uncle Ben I was wearing the mink coat. When we told them about our plans to do a lot of camping Ben asked, "In a fur coat?" I explained that on cool, damp nights in the tent it would make a great extra blanket.

We stayed with dear old friend, Duane, from Bob's animation class. He brought champagne to the ship, and suggested he might rent himself out as a Professional Waver. He said he could charge $10 with champagne; $15 to include "Oh, don't go, PLEASE DON'T GO!; $25 to jump in and swim after the boat.

We stayed on deck just long enough to pass the Statue

of Liberty. Our cabin has no porthole, and even if it did, I couldn't have looked out; the next 24 hours of "heavy swells" were grim indeed. I, at least, had the decency to stay in my bunk suffering quietly, but not Bob. He felt he had to struggle up on deck, clutching his brown urpies bag, wandering around disposing of his meals hither and yon. "It's much better to eat", he kept telling me. "I met Peter. Peter's a sailor, and he says you should eat". Peter should meet Bob's grandmother.

Suddenly, three days later, a miracle happened. I got out of bed to go to the toilet, and the toilet sat there. STILL.

Bob recovered about the same time, as did the rest of the ship, and seeing 90% of the passengers as green and pale as we were, I no longer felt any stigma or need to apologize for having spent the past 72 hours in bed.

Once up I began to discover the real life On Board. At 6 PM each day a walking starched apron comes rapping at the door to announce, "Your bahth is ready, Madame". (Imagine, me a Madame already) I trip down the corridor to a private room with a steaming bahth, fresh bar of soap and heated towel awaiting my pleasure.

Then comes eating. I had thought that Bob's grandmother had a corner on the catering biz, but even she would feel humble next to the Holland American Line chef. I must have gained ten pounds on the "Chantilly" alone. Everything arrives "a la Chantilly", which is whipped cream, as in real whipped cream like we used to have and rarely find anymore. No ersatz here. The pure sweet cream, butter, cheese, milk, fresh fruit, freshly baked bread, wafers, pastry, and four-count-em-four desserts forces me to say a silent prayer before every meal (and the constant "snacks") in which I plead for some kind of self-restraint and/or that clothes are very cheap abroad. I have, in the short space of four eating days, outgrown everything I own with the exception of a single black sweater dress which can still accommodate a few more bulges.

I might have made it through all right, desserts included, but for the fact that the Palm Court offers lovely drinks at around 25 cents apiece, so that one dollar carries us way past our normal bedtime, and if we splurge, we can stay up half the night with all our other new friends, which we have been doing every night. How many useless calories are there in a cognac?

We're in no hurry for the trip to end, and what with the "moderate swells" we've been having, I doubt we'll make up all that time we lost during the "heavy swells" the first 48 hours out of New York.

I'll stop for now because these "moderate swells" may well make it impossible for you to read this.

Contentedly,
C & B

Addendum - April 22nd, PM

We spotted some small islands earlier this morning and spent most of the day watching the ships and planes which passed more frequently as we neared the English coast. The seagulls following the ship are beautiful.

We're now anchored in the Channel outside of Southampton. We'll dock there in the AM just long enough to discharge passengers and mail, then go on to Le Havre. Tomorrow night? Paris!

I would say that I was still sea-sick, except that Peter, our resident expert on all matters pertaining to sea voyages, tells us it is another syndrome completely: Channel Fever.

I could hardly eat the main dessert at the farewell dinner tonight, but it did look exciting - almost pure chocolate whipped cream, with just enough cake under it to keep it decent. They offered us seconds, but, of course, I refused. I'd like to be able to waddle ashore at least, under my own power, and not have to be wheeled around Europe.

Excitedly,
C & B

P.S. We're sending you some photos of us taken on board. Well, at least my shoes still fit.

4

Arrival

April 23, 1959

The landing at Le Havre was beautiful! Far from being an oil-soaked bay with dirty docks, such as we from Southern California know and don't love, the water is deep green. The surrounding wall is very old, grey-black brick, crumbled in parts from all the wars it must have seen. Most of all, everything is quiet, almost hushed, as the motors of the ship were turned off and tugs pulled us in.

It took over an hour to enter the port. We stood on the bridge and took photos of all the other ships passing to and fro, and the beach, which was full of school-boys waving at us. Thursday is a school holiday in France.

Actually, we almost didn't make it ashore. The anticipation of docking was too much for us, giddy as we were from a sleepless night brought on, no doubt, by the Channel Fever Peter warned us about. Besides we had a last minute panic when we started packing and realized not only we, but our suitcases as well, had gained weight, thanks to a full set of large, handsome menus as proof that all that Chantilly wasn't an exaggeration. Add a few bottles of Peach Liqueur at tax free prices, and copies of the ship's Daily News; we couldn't possibly get everything in. So there we were, hunting up old shopping bags and into "hand luggage" yet again, to give us once more, appropriately enough, that sincere immigrant look.

The excitement of docking was fierce: hurried, emotional good-byes, as we tripped down the gangplank, not so lightly, of course, and one of us shouted, "Well, gang, we're almost there!" only to have the two French guards look at us and in very bad English tell us we must have landing cards.

We, in turn, told them in worse French that they were crazy. We had passports, and health certificates, and vaccination scars and shots, and as we babbled on incoherently, the other passengers tried to tell us that they were issuing landing cards on deck. So we turned around and marched back on board, almost in tears. All this trouble and they wouldn't let us into France. We finally got the darned landing cards and struggled back as far as the gangplank when Bob said that he had lost his. We had to turn around again and retrace our steps until we found the battered, but still living, landing card. Customs was a breeze. Very sweet, the French, winking at all the girls.

We boarded the boat-train, it tooted its whistle, and from that moment on we haven't dared to blink for fear of missing something. (I will never, never be able to follow Dr. Hare's advice to keep my glasses off, in order to improve my myopia.)

And right here and now let me tell you those impressionists were a bunch of fakes. Van Gogh included. Original, my eye, myopic or otherwise. They just took their paint boxes and stools out into these fields and copied!

The more we saw the more we became babbling idiots.

When the sight of a Frenchman wearing a blue beret riding a bicycle home with a loaf of unwrapped "French" to us, normal to him, bread under his arms sent us into raptures of excitement, I knew we were way over the edge of reason.

Everything went perfectly: we arrived around eight o'clock, just as the lights and all those fountains were being turned on; we had a perfectly insane cab driver, as we had every right to have, who swerved and braked and sped and honked, as he barely missed whatever was in his path, all the way. Glorious! And as luck would also have it, our hotel was on the other side of the Seine so we had a cheap tour of the city in the bargain.

Here's another What if? Once on the left bank we were let out in front of "un petit hotel". Do you remember my mentioning that we had a hotel room reserved for us in Paris? Do you remember by whom? Those old friends who had toured Europe a couple of years ago, and by the end of their trip in Paris, with almost no money left had found "a real find hotel"? They could recommend it highly. Only trouble was that the first morning there the maid knocked on their door to ask, "One breakfast or two"? They later found out it was what is called a "Hotel de Passe" where the local streetwalkers use the rooms by the hour, give or take a few minutes. But our friends said the owner was sweet and charming, and after all, it was only $1.50 a night, including breakfast.

So we were prepared for something less than luxurious. However, when the door opened and we were greeted by a wild apparition carrying a telephone and wearing a pink plastic hat with a giant tube attaching it and her to something in the other room, while a wolf-dog barked and salivated at her feet, (luckily he was hung up in all the cords and couldn't get to us), we were somewhat startled.

Back to the Fractured French again. Yes, she was the owner-please forgive her-her hair in the dryer (oh, was that what it was?) and all. No, she didn't have a double room for us, but could get us one next door. Yes, she had a single room for our friend, but not until 10 o'clock that night, did he want it for "<u>all</u>" night? (This was Jim, whom we had met on board, and whom I had talked out of landing in England as he had planned, ["You must see Paris!"] so I felt responsible for him).

Later, we climbed five flights of stairs (no elevator), which were barely covered by a what once, some eons ago, might have passed for a maroon "runner", and struggled into a tiny room with just the inventory contained in my vocabulary list: a bed (masc.sing.); a chair; a tiny table; a washbasin, another kind of basin mounted in a stand close to the floor, (oh,sure "bidet") and at last I understood the noun (another masc. singular) "Armoire a glace." I was told it was the French answer to the closet problem. I suppose it is if you just have one shirt and one pair of shoes. There was, to complete the furnishings, a 25 watt bulb glued somehow to the ceiling.

Still, when I opened the window, (French doors, what else?) and took one look at all those old roof-tops and orange chimney pots shining in the moonlight, we were hooked. Suddenly everything was charming and beautiful, and weren't they right when they said "In Paris there is something "dans l'aire"?!

All we needed was to walk over to the Place de la Concorde and I was sure we'd find Gene Kelly and Leslie Caron dancing their hearts out.

Thrilled Beyond Belief,
C & B

5

Paris

Well, start packing. This must be the most beautiful city in the world, but you'll just have to come see it for yourselves.

French onion soup in the Eiffel Tower! Glorious! We wandered from level to level, took photos of all the views; I even fell in love with the potted plants in the flower-box we discovered amidst the machinery, oil, and debris in the maintenance area on the third level. Shows how far gone we are. We're simply encapsulated in a cloud of enchantment.

However, if anything will bring us back to reality, it will be the toilets. After the first shock of finding that le toilet is, apart from grammar, masculine <u>and</u> feminine, I've stopped looking for His and Hers. Actually, it's rather nice to have someone take off his hat and wish you Bon Jour when you walk into le toilet.

No, it's the paper. I know we were warned, but we carry so much as it is...still, I'm liable to be scarred for life. They say that France is the only country where you can't tear the toilet paper and the money falls apart in your hands.

Then there are bidets. They seem to be almost a religious object. Everything else can be in all stages of disrepair, but by golly, there is always a bright and shiny bidet sparkling before your very eyes. Yes, even in the public restrooms. Makes me wonder, what could one (feminine) be doing in a bar needing a bidet? By the way, the restrooms are more often referred to as the Water Closet, abbreviated to W.C. but how do you pronounce "W.C." in French?) I hope we're here long enough for me to get over this particular cultural shock.

Speaking of cultural shock, at least now we don't wander the streets commenting on how many foreign cars there are around. Nor look into a grocery window and whistle at the amount of imported foods.

Speaking of which, you won't catch me slobbering all over the paper trying to tell you about the food either. I'll just say this: we're still eating much too much. Never really having recovered from the meals on board ship, we were thrown face to face with "croissants." They may look like ordinary crescent breakfast rolls, but have you ever eaten crescent shaped breakfast rolls made of hundreds of buttery layers of delicate dough, barely tinged with sugared goodness?

Our first morning we had breakfast in a cafe. The waiter brought us a basket full of croissants, and we ate all but two. Bob said well, maybe he could eat another, after all, we'll have to pay for them. We stuffed our overblown cheeks some more, and the waiter came and did a double take. "How many did we eat?" he asked. We didn't know. After all, one can't keep track of everything. Then he explained that one is only charged for what one eats, and we watched as he refilled the basket and took the same basket over to another table where there were waiting customers. We'll have to rethink our standards of sanitation. But looking around no one looked any less heathy than we. Thinner too. It was only then I saw the owner's cat sitting on the food counter.

One afternoon we decided to do our own grocery shopping and have dinner in our room, mainly because I've wanted to walk home with an unwrapped French bread under my arm. Then, at last, I would have convinced myself that I was in France.

We bought cheese, fruit, wine, and the bread. And what we thought would have been a problem-that is buying just enough for one meal, turned out to be a way of life. There are few refrigerators here, and if there were, I still get the feeling everyone would buy just enough for each meal. Voila: One can get 50 grams of butter, 100 grams of cheese, one egg, one small paper cone of cherries, one orange and, I suppose, one grape if you so desired.

We stopped to buy some violets too. How can one sit down to a meal of good French cheese, French bread, French wine, French fruit, without French flowers?

We opened the windows in our room to let the moonlight in, took deep breaths of the fresh spring air of Paris, unlike anything we've known before, and sat down at our tiny table with our not so tiny feast. Our cup runneth over.

We still have Versailles and Sacre Coeur, Jeu de Paume, parts of the Louvre, and the Crazy Horse Saloon to do, not necessarily in that order. You may think we haven't accomplished much in our two weeks here but it is a bit difficult to take care of our business when we no more than get up and out, raring to go, only to find everything shutting down around us at twelve sharp for lunch, not to open again until two, sometimes three. By then we're hungry (we couldn't very well eat lunch at twelve when we finished breakfast with lots of croissants, at eleven), but all the restaurants are closed, never to open their doors again until seven or eight. The bars take pity on us and we get our choice of a cheese or ham sandwich, which we're forced to gulp down in order to get back to those places above which will close down again at seven-thirty.

We've been trying to pick up our car for days, as we should get on the road to Cannes for the Film Festival. With our official letter from the University of California Press, stating that we represent their "Film Quarterly" magazine, we managed to get accreditation and press passes. Another Big What If- More later.

Sloppily,
C & B

BONUS CARD! BONUS CARD!

We're at the International Flower Show, the Floralie, just outside the city, held in yet another exciting architectural structure: a poured concrete slanting roof which drains beautifully. We know because it hasn't stopped raining since we arrived. The show is unbelievable-they have dragged in large trees, made ponds and pools, and transplanted entire groves of flowers and vegetables. I never realized what creative displays a creative mind could dream up using only cucumbers and turnips!

They also have exhibits of stamps, tapestries, paintings, books, magazines, all with flowers as subject matter. All the advertising, food, and other commercial nonsense is off to one side, in an unobtrusive area, adding greatly to the general charm and ambiance.

There are thousands of people here, on a normal work day, which makes us wonder how many people would turn out for a flower show in Los Angeles on a Tuesday?

But the biggest thrill of the day is that we just gave directions to a lost Frenchman-in French! Not only that, he understood us!

Smugly,
C & B

6

Enroute Cannes

We finally managed to pick up our brand new Peugeot 403. What we had been dreading as yet another foray into the bureaucratic maelstrom turned out to be an unbelievable example of French efficiency.

The address on our instructions wasn't as obscure as it sounded, and when we entered the elegant-but-way-past-its prime, massive, 19th century building, the concierge took one look at us and, very bored, pointed to a door off the main courtyard. I guess we still look very much like American tourists-we're certainly fatter than all these svelte and sleek Parisians, and then there are my sneakers which I just can't seem to give up.

Our hearts dropped as we walked in and saw a few more bored men behind a long counter and in back of them, in this enormous room, dozens and dozens of rickety shelves filled with what looked like hundreds and hundreds of un-tidy packets, each held together with rubber bands. Bob muttered a not so quiet aside, "This will take days!"

We shoved our papers over to one of the men who hardly bothered to look at them, walked over to the nearest shelf, pulled down one of the packets, took off the rubber band, motioned for us to sign one of the papers, rubber-stamped a couple more, handed us back our papers, along with a couple of new ones, and told us, in French, to go pick up our car in the back.

Total Time: two and one-half minutes.

In another ten we were heading into Paris traffic in our beautiful, blue, 1959 Peugeot 403 (Quatre Cents Trois, pronounced "Cat Sahn Twah." If you're going to own one, you had better be able to say it. A good friend here told us he always tries to take a Peugeot taxi because he loves to ask the driver how he likes his Peugeot, knowing that invariably the driver will pat the seat lovingly and with great emotion answer, "Tres Solide" (solid), "Tray Soleed!"

I know reams have been written about Paris traffic, but let me tell you, that is not nearly enough. Take the right-of-way syndrome. They <u>really mean</u> that the car on the right has the right of way. Always. A car can come barging out of any side street and roar into traffic, providing only that it's on the right. It can turn from any lane, cross over any way the driver chooses, yielding only to any car on *its* right. There may be some sense in all this, but to us it's sheer madness.

Pedestrians have no status. One must learn to chase them down, thus one takes one's life in one's hands crossing any street on foot. We could find only two traffic signals in Paris, and they really don't count since there's a policeman there directing traffic any way he sees fit. And what he sees fit doesn't necessarily coincide with the signal.

To make things complete, throughout the city they have these "Etoile" or roundabouts where surrounding streets radiate in all directions, like those amusement park rides where the cars break away and spin off-except there they only spin off in one direction.

Night driving brings its own terrors. One is <u>only</u> allowed to use dim, yellow parking lights when driving in Paris at night. When one approaches an intersection, and one only knows it is an intersection because of a small yellow light buried in the macadam, one is supposed to flash one's lights, and of course, depending on whether one is on the right or left, charge through accordingly.

Actually, this is Bob's favorite free-form style of driving, swerving in and charging out; I just try to look the other way.

Yet another problem is finding a gas station. I suppose much of what makes Paris such a beautiful city is that all power lines, telephone and otherwise, are buried underground. We began to think that ugly gas stations might be as well. More discreet they couldn't be, and the only good part about all this is that when you finally find one, hugging its tiny space up against an otherwise attractive building, the relief is so great you're willing to forgive its modesty.

Much as we hated to leave Paris, it was a bit of a relief to get on roads where all we had to worry about was the speed of the cars constantly trying to overtake us, and making room for them to pass. We thought we were making good time, but not according to all the French drivers who flashed their lights, passing us as if we were standing still. They probably got their basic training in Paris.

The other problem was again trying to find gas stations. We kept missing them for all the tulips planted in and around the pumps. Not only that, but their oil cans are white transparent plastic and <u>*clean!*</u> Once we stopped looking for flying flags and dirty pumps, and realized that small flower-filled arbors with a shaded table and chairs waiting to be occupied for a rest and aperitif signified a gas station, we were fine. The attendants smile when you ask them where the W.C. is, and when you come back to the car they drop everything to open the door, adjust your skirt so it won't catch in the door, and sing out as you leave, "Au revoir, Madame!"

We spent our first night in Tournus, in a charming inn which had been built onto the walls of what had been an old Romanesque church. It was like a large private home; we went in through the back, right to our room, and later, in the restaurant, we registered. There was no reception desk as such, and every time we went back and forth from our room to the restaurant and lounge we had to go through the kitchen.

No, I won't tell you about the food. I can't do it without slobbering,

C & B

P.S. I've discovered perfume. We went into a perfume shop on the Champs-Elysées to find a little something for Bob's Mom's birthday, and I almost swooned. No wonder I turned up my nose, literally, all these years. This was nothing like the stringent, artificial "eau d' whatever", we have, even at Saks. No the scent in these vials has the very essence of freshly blooming precious flowers. I also bought a wee vial for myself too. If the shower shortage keeps up I'm going to need a lot more, budget be damned.

7

Cannes

Well, what with all the time we spent finding gas stations and dawdling in beautiful old inns, we were a few days late arriving in Cannes and, as luck and habit would have it, we got here at 11:45, just in time for everything to close for lunch. To convince ourselves we were actually on the "French Riviera" we wandered along the Croisette looking at the blue Mediterranean (me) and all the girls in their bikinis (Bob). Lunch on the terrace of the famous Blue Bar was even more convincing.

FLASHBACK:

A very big WHAT IF? A week or so before we were to leave, we were at the UCLA Animation Dept. to check on one of the three films Bob made and were in their archives. By chance we ran into Ernie Callenbach, the editor of Film Quarterly. We told him we were leaving for France shortly, and he asked if we were going to the Cannes Festival? We hadn't thought of it, actually, but he said he would give us a letter of introduction to their press office and if we did, and if we sent him a few reviews he'd publish them in Film

Quarterly. And that is how we got to this year's Cannes Festival!

We finally got our press cards stamped, and were given a folder full of programs, film publicity, etc. With a good dictionary I might be able to translate the French by the end of summer.

We managed, amazingly, to find a cheap hotel in this very expensive town and soon settled down to the exhausting life of cinema journalists. After breakfast in bed we would lie on the beach and swim for a couple of hours (Aside: Yes, I bought a bikini-there are no other bathing suits available, then spent two hours sewing four inch eyelets around the top and bottom. It helped, but each time I wear it, I still feel the same as when I disrobe in a doctor's office: take a deep breath and just go on hold.

Then, there's a two-hour lunch. We're tired of being scoffed at as "Crazy Americans who rush through dejeuner." The French see this haste as a highway to death by liver ailment. I don't know, if it's a liver ailment we're to die of, it won't be from indigestion but from all the wine we're drinking.

Around three we wander into a matinee. Once we realized there were no simultaneous translations-you should have seen us at first scrambling around under the seats looking for non-existent earphones-and at best all we could expect was French sub-titles, we settled down to tense concentration, trying to figure out what each film was about. It's definitely a challenge, and in a couple of cases, having read the synopsis later, I felt the story I had made up was much better. If our reviews turn out to be a bit vague, I'll know the reason why.

Then it's coffee and the six o'clock showing of the main feature. We can't get into the gala 9:00 screening because

Bob doesn't have a "Smoking", (what we call a tuxedo.) However, learning about the "Smoking" problem, a very nice Finnish reporter, insisting that all Bob needed was a black bow-tie to get us into the formal late showings, took us into town and supervised the purchase. I kept protesting, "A black silk bow-tie with his Brooks Bros. <u>brown</u> drip-dry suit?" We only dared try it on rainy nights because then Bob could wear his raincoat. I arranged it so that all any official could see was the bow-tie and his ears.

Anyhow, on most nights we don't have to rush through dinner like "Crazy Americans." It's getting so I just don't feel right if I can't reserve a full two hours to negotiate my bifteck.

Languidly,
C & B

Fast Forward: Another 'as luck would have it," it rained the last night of the festival and we could partake of all the glamour: many named stars, lots of Movietone news cameras, or the equivalent thereof: what must have been all the police in the south of France recruited for the occasion and standing at attention next to their scooters (no motorcycles), capes flying in the rain; lots of Rolls Royces. Good old-fashioned pizazz.

We lingered outside, waiting to see Mille Perkins arrive and make her entrance- "The Diary Of Anne Frank" was the closing film"-before we rushed into the salon (not "theater", dope). By then the only seats left were in the second row, which was reserved for the stars, but things were rather confused, and the usual ushers frantic just seconds before the lights dimmed, so we just slipped in. It was nice to be so close except that meant we couldn't remove our raincoats. Lucky thing too, we were in every newsreel in France last week. I wanted to wave, but Bob said we were conspicuous enough as it was, huddled in our raincoats.

Later, as we were sitting at a sidewalk café on the Croisette, having our nightcap, FOOM! FEU D'ARTIFICE! Fireworks! They were firing from the beach across the street out over the water. And such a display! It was just like the scene in "To Catch A Thief", where you see the fireworks through the window of the Cannes Carlton Hotel as Grace Kelly and Cary Grant smooch in the foreground.

Well, here we were, right next to the Carlton, Cary Grant was in town, Grace Kelly was just down the road, and there were these glorious fireworks!

Suitably Impressed,
C & B

Further report from the outfield in Cannes:

Most of the festival participants were invited by the Mayor of Cannes to a luncheon on one of the nearby islands, and somehow l) we received an invitation and 2) were able to figure out what it said.

And…if I hadn't seen it with my very own eyes…as soon as we all got off the boat, several of the girls plunged into the water. Dozens of photographers gathered around and tried to encourage one of the aging starlets to take off her bikini. After a few weak "demurrals", she agreed to take off her top and substitute two soup ladles one of the waiters had gaily provided. Well, it wasn't too long before soup was served and the ladles were required elsewhere. Next thing I knew, standing there sipping my Pernod, attempting nonchalance, in my very proper orange silk Saks skirt and blouse-to-match (how was I supposed to know the lunch was *on the beach* of "the island"?) someone had picked up Little Miss Undress, carried her over to a rock, and "struggled" to separate her bikini bottom from her own rather large bottom, as dozens of photographers appeared out of nowhere, bumping into mothers dragging their kids away.

I turned around to ask Bob if he saw what I saw, and no Bob! Looking back to the scene of all this frivolity, THERE he was, up to his knees in water, pants getting saltier by the minute, but a wet pair of slacks is a small price to pay for the best seat, so to speak, in the house.

Aside: At least his ear is healing nicely, the one he bashed day before yesterday. He's monitor of our press mailbox, and his duty every morning is to run down to the Palais de Festival, pick up all the bulletins of the day, talk to the other journalists, find out the latest gossip about which stars are due to arrive, and how many girls PLAYBOY magazine is shooting nude on the beach at 5 AM every morning, and like that.

Well, once back on the Croisette, along the beach, apparently he was eyes left, toward the bikinis, on a collision course with a banner pole, ear level, and came back with blood pouring down his neck. It took quite a while to get him cleaned up and the story straight, and I made him promise to look at the lady sunbathers only while standing still.

On the way back from the island to the mainland, we shared a small boat with Hugh Hefner, some of his PLAYBOY staff, and Allan Ginsberg. We compared notes on some of the films. They didn't understand the subtitles either. Evidently Hefner and his crew are covering, (or uncovering) the festival, from the point of view of the girls, of course. I suggested they title it "Boobies on the Rocks"....

The next day, "Le Scandale" exploded. Newspapers were filled with photos of our Lady of the Ladles, as well as indignant protests, official and otherwise. "Is this a cultural event or is it not?" It took three press conferences, with personal appearances of M. Le Directeur, and the lady herself, fully dressed as Mother Hubbard, in tears, trying to explain how 1) she is a very serious actress and 2) she was forced to remove her top. It was at this point, as I recall, that the mayor himself put his arm around her and asked all of us press folk present if this wasn't a perfect example of a victim of over zealous journalism. It was a touching performance and we were all suitably chastened and left the salle, many of us wondering out loud if the head of the Press Department was hinting that if anyone insisted on prolonging this most unfortunate affair, his/her press pass would be revoked. Tempest In A Soup Ladle?

The festival ends in a couple of days, but we may not be leaving yet. Flashback: More advice from Mark, my old hairdresser in LA (remember his previous advice re: the Maasdam, etc, gathered from his recent trips to Europe?). "If you ever go to Cannes, you must look up my old client, Phyllis."

And so we did, inviting her and her mother to one of the screenings; they were enthralled, never having been to anything at the festival, after which they insisted we come over to their villa in nearby Juan Les Pins for lunch.

And so we did. Phyllis is an old around 50 and her mother a young around 80, who when the doctor warned her to cut down on those three manhattans she has every night before dinner, she did. "Only one" she said, smiling, "But I have it in a highball glass".

Our lunch began on the terrace with lots of champagne and casual conversation. By the time we moved to the garden for a seven course meal, each with copious goblets of the appropriate wines, it became easier and easier to be our most charming selves.

Later they wanted to teach us how to play *chemin de fer*, sort of a complicated blackjack-so we'd know all about it when they took us to the casino. Yes, they insisted we come right out after the festival to spend at least a week with them. "We won't take no for an answer". Who was going to argue?

So when next you hear from us, we'll likely be sipping more champagne, popping caviar into our big, fat mouths, sunning on the terrace of a Riviera villa on the Cote D'Azur.....

Hardly Containably,
C & B

P.S. Just so you don't think all is luxurious splendor, let me tell you about our hotel room here, and how not to believe everything you read in guide books. First, the bed: oh, it's a real, whole bed this time, but the spring part is enormous and covered with a plastic sheet with a "printed• eyelet design. The mattress is rather thin, the sort they use on cots in institutions. Finally, the sheets, and I wish I could cut off a piece of the material to send you, are almost canvas: unbleached, unfinished, the flax nubs still sharp. It's the next "best" thing to sleeping on sandpaper. And I still can't get used to the sheet winding up and around a rather hard bolster which is stretched across the width of the bed and is supposed to be a pillow. It is, I guess, except that it is unmovable, being integrated completely into the sheet. But because it's France, I still think it's charming.

Now, all the guide books tell you <u>never</u> to get a room with a bath, because rooms with baths are so rare and so

expensive, and every hotel <u>always</u> has at least one bathroom available on each floor, so why pay extra for a private one? Remember, bathrooms are for bathing only. Le
Toilette is always separate.

Well, this may not be a typical hotel but after we made
a great scene about not wanting a room with a bath, we
later found out they have only four rooms <u>without</u> a bath,
one of which we were in, and what's more, there is no other
bathroom available for those four rooms.

Sponging helped for the first few days, but frankly by
now we're beginning to ignore each other and politely trying to sit at opposite ends of the room, out of courtesy and
respect....

Fragrantly yours,
C & B

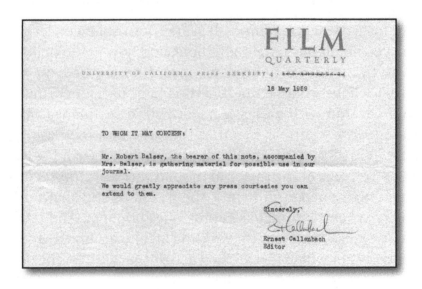

FILM
QUARTERLY

UNIVERSITY OF CALIFORNIA PRESS · BERKELEY 4 ·

18 May 1959

TO WHOM IT MAY CONCERN:

Mr. Robert Balser, the bearer of this note, accompanied by
Mrs. Balser, is gathering material for possible use in our
journal.

We would greatly appreciate any press courtesies you can
extend to them.

Sincerely,

Ernest Callenbach
Editor

Hotel bill Cannes

8

Villa Sans Souci ("Without Worry")

Once away from the Film Festival racket we tottered out to Cap D'Antibes and Villa Sans Souci. Phyllis and Mama are from an old Boston book-publishing company and have lived in Europe on and off (on between wars; off during wars) since Phyllis was a child. Father was left home with his books and stamp collection. "He preferred a quiet life after he retired at 25".

They hate "Niggers, Jews, Roosevelt ("He was a wicked, wicked man"), Frenchmen, Austrians, and the Swiss, in that order. They like their two Pekingese and Italians, also in that order.

At first we could find no graceful way of pulling out without jeopardizing Mark's relationship with these people. Then it started to rain, and we started to write our reviews, thinking it would only take a day or two. But it turned out to be hard work, mostly because we kept arguing over the plots. *"He did too kill his wife." "That wasn't his wife, dummy, it was his half-sister, don't you remember the guy who came in with the gun? THAT was her uncle!"*

Well, <u>you</u> try to figure out a Bulgarian film with French sub-titles.

The other problem with our new careers as film critics was that even though we were good, (read *compulsive),* about sitting through all the clunkers, of course, maybe if we had understood them their overall merits might have improved), we somehow missed the best film of the Festival, "400 Blows". We may never live this down in the years to come. Does it help if we sat through "Black Orpheus" twice?

It took us six days to finish our work. This antagonized Phyllis no end because what's the sense of having houseguests if they don't perform 24 hours a day? The fact that it rained most of the time didn't sooth her ruffled feathers.

We were beginning to compile our own list of hates, such as the two Pekingese ("Toyse-Woysie" and "Pee-Wee" want to go outsie-poutsie? Well, then get on harney-warney") - who would think nothing of snarling and trying to bite off any finger wanting to pet (or strangle) them, as they attached themselves to any stray leg for rubsie uppie-downie.

Since Phyllis consumes a fifth of gin a day before dinner, then switches to brandy highballs for the rest of the night, by bedtime she was pretty outsie-poutsie too. We thought we were being rather gracious when we first arrived and along with the flowers, gave her a bottle of brandy. She took it casually enough, tossed off a quick "Oh, thanks", and set it down next to two magnums on the buffet. Barely a week's supply as it turned out.

At one point, trying to express her horror at the amount of coffee Americans drink, she said, "Jesus, they drink coffee like it was cocktails, or something!!!"

Toysie and Pee-Wee aren't totally housebroken, as it turns out, but Phyllis doesn't seem to mind picking up the occasional turd or mopping up the morning puddles.

She's totally devoted to them, maybe because they are such lookalikes, she and they. You know how sometimes pets resemble their owners? Well, just picture your typical Pekingese, and you have our Phyllis.

The most common cuss word in French is, of course, "merde", literally "shit". But we were told that nice young girls and ladies prefer "crotte", or dog droppings, which for some reason or another, they consider more refined, which in turn may or may not account for Phyllis's attitude.

Our other hate was Chemin de Fer. You remember how I wrote that we had learned to play with matchsticks? And how at the end of that first afternoon Bob had won all the matchsticks?

Well, one night Phyllis dragged us to the Casino. She went most nights, but had held back in deference to us and the budget we tried to explain we were working on. We didn't have the courage however, to tell her it was only $300 a month, not enough to even cover her liquor bill. She and Mama thought it was all very quaint and courageous of us, camping and all that.

Anyhow, off we went to the Casino. Bob even had hopes of a small killing, and that is exactly what it turned out to be - a very quick and merciless murder of two of our precious $10 and one $5 travelers' checks, all in the space of ten minutes.

Seems as if the cards they use in the Casino aren't numbered in all the familiar corners. So unless one is familiar with the system, as Bob was not, instead of counting everyone else's cards and plays, at which he is pretty good, he was trying to count the hearts, diamonds, spades and clubs on each and every card. That along with the shock of the speed and efficiency of the croupier and other players, is something to behold, at a distance if possible. Bob didn't even know it was his play before it was all over, and his pitiful pile of chips was all over too.

We were both too stunned to do much more the rest of the evening than wander around getting bigger and better electric shocks on those thick, plushy rugs.

The only funny part of the whole trauma was Phyllis running into one of her friends who was trying to drown her sorrow in drink and cards. Her husband had run away with another woman to Switzerland, cashing $7,000 worth of bad checks before he left, checks the banks were after her to make good. The real tragedy, she explained, was that he had also taken her two poodles. "How are they going to get their pedicures every week?" she sobbed, "You know how careless he is about things like that!"

Actually, we got to know a bit more of the local life and color of the Riviera expat crowd, as anyone new is to be shown off as much as possible, and we obliged Phyllis by following her around town. Here is a typical day: Phyllis and Mama have breakfast in bed and an hour of double deck solitaire. At 10 they dress and totter down with their baskets and the Pekingese to shop at the open-air market. Then come aperitifs in the cafe where the local expats meet to compare last evening's Casino losses, and who has done what to whom. (Latest news on the run-away husband: he's still in Switzerland. Apparently Interpol is sleeping on the job.)

If it's lunch at home, Phyllis changes into her bikini. It's not that she is terribly overweight, it's just that all the bulges are in the wrong places, such as her buddha belly overhanging the bottom part of her bikini which surely must be lurking down there somewhere. She's not at all self-conscious about wandering about like this, and if nothing else, her nonchalance is to be admired. Mama sticks to proper old-fashioned light-weight print dresses, sunhat, and where it can't be avoided-steep cobblestoned hills, for example-a cane.

So it's onto the terrace to water a few plants before lunch, and then initiate the day's serious drinking, which will not have any real interruptions until bedtime. More aperitifs, wine with lunch, of course, sometimes a token coffee, sometimes not.

There is usually a brief siesta before a quick change for another trip to town for "errands." These are really an excuse to go to one outdoor cafe or another to watch the world go by and meet up again with the expat society, which may or may not, depending on the time of month and Casino luck, regroup for dinner out. Phyllis and Mama's favorite is The Blue Bar on the Croisette in Cannes. "They love Toysie and Pee-Wee and take such good care of them." (I'll say. They got the same gold-rimmed plates as we, with what looked like a slightly better cut of roast beef, all handed down to them under the table by a white-gloved waiter). Then it's on to the Casino.

One afternoon a week, there is bridge, and sometimes, when there are out of town guests, brief excursions are made in the nearby countryside. One day we were taken to charming Eze, where we stopped for coffee at the famous Le Chèvre d'Or and and saw Simone Signoret holding court at the head of a long table filled with very attractive young men. How the French men adore "mature women"!

A very important part of Phyllis and Mama's schedule always includes, at some point during the year, always month in Rome, just to stay at the Majestic Hotel.

When I asked Mama, of all the places they had lived in Europe which she liked the most, expecting a city, town, or village for an answer, she replied, "Oh, without a doubt, the Majestic Hotel in Rome."

I think it was at this point that we felt it was time to bid fond adieu to Villa Sans Souci...

Fondly?
C & B

P.S. Before we left, Phyllis advised me to keep "a log" of each day's activities. "It will be very useful as you travel"

9

Back to Paris

It took us most of an entire day to pack up again. That mink coat seems to have some self expanding mechanism taking up more and more room as we move along. We hug, kiss, and thank Phyllis and Mama. They had been after all, extremely generous, and we'll never forget the view from our room: down the hill through the pine trees, the sparkling blue Mediterranean, upon which there always seemed to be a white sailboat, making a perfect composition for the perfect postcard.

I think they were sorry to see us leave. Once we finished our writing chores and agreed to stay another week (no great sacrifice), now available for fun and games, I guess that evened up the score as far as they were concerned. They kept telling everyone what a "cute couple" we were and wasn't it adventurous all this camping we were going to do?

We also had to say goodbye to Marie and her Swiss husband, Albert, the live-in couple. They liked us a lot, perhaps because, as they told us, we were the only guests who ever made their own beds and picked up their own clothes.

We didn't leave until after four- "It's so late now, you may as well stay for lunch, Marie has made her special Semola Gateau..." But we were still determined to start camping that very night, to begin making up for our heavy losses in the Casino, and logged all of ten miles before we stopped in Grasse, the perfume capital of the world.

Aside: I keep forgetting to tell you about the ubiquitous string bag. Everyone carries one kind or another of this marvel of efficiency, in any pocket, handbag or briefcase, ready to be produced when needed to carry any and all purchases. When one buys two oranges, one is handed two oranges, no packages are provided, but no problem: along with any other purchases, they go into the string bag, which expands to accommodate a surprising amount of shopping.

So we bought a string bag, one-burner butane Gaz stove, one big pot, one dish towel, bread, cheese, and wine. Then we followed the arrows on the "Camping" signs-good international word, "Camping", and parked in a big grassy field, ours was the only car, it is still May, remember. Next, we retrieved the Peugeot manual and figured out how to fold back the front seats to connect with the back seats to make a bed. This particular feature was what decided us, after giving up the idea of trying to bicycle, or scooter, through Europe (what if it rains?) on the Peugeot. "Think of all the fun it will be, sleeping in the car!"

We rolled out the air mats and sleeping bags we had shipped to the Maasdam and had been carrying with us since then, threw them across the stretched out seats, and voila, we were camping.

And freezing. But we stood there and ate our bread, cheese, and wine and tried not to compare this dinner with what Phyllis, Mama, Toysie-Woysie, and Pee-Wee were having at The Blue Bar.

We quickly decided that we needed additional supplies, such as a small camp table and stools, a sharp knife, plus ceramic mugs. We had also shipped our old aluminum mess kits but I had forgotten how hot coffee in an aluminum cup burns your lips. I also vowed to keep the mink coat handy (I *said* it could be used as an auxiliary blanket.)

The only other problem we had was getting used to the toilets. Being an old camper, and familiar with the ubiquitous shacks with wooden planks, hole in the center, over a very smelly chemical something or other in our National Parks, I was prepared for just about anything. Anything, that is, except two foot-shaped porcelain floor plates placed strategically over a slightly indented hole in the middle.

Actually, these are rather common, and since then I've become quite expert in their use. You walk in, take your stand-up position on the two plates, (some of the fancier ones even have shoe sole patterns stamped on the metal or porcelain), use the hole in the middle, then pull the chain and leave. Only trouble is, when you pull some chains, the water rushes in at flood-level, and if you've made the mistake of staying on the plates, you can easily get bathed, from bottom up to the ankles. The other problem is that some of them have automatic flush. The first time this happened, you can imagine how I felt, trapped on the plates when the flood started. My sneakers will never be the same.

Now I open the door cautiously, wait at least 20 seconds to see if it is A.F. (Automatic Flush.) If so, I count the number of seconds between flooding times, and make sure I get out of the way in time. If, however, it's a manual chain-flush, I finish, grab the chain, get as close to the door as possible and on tip-toes, pull, and run like hell. Anyhow, with all that gushing water they're a lot cleaner than those wooden planks.

After all that our first camping experience entailed (see above) what better place to be than Grasse. We did the traditional things, such as smell the air, heavily perfumed with the flowers that grow profusely over hill and dale; visit the perfume factories (Did you know it takes four to five tons of flower petals to make one kilo of essence? No wonder, etc.). I even splurged on a rouge-size pat of perfumed wax. Good for traveling, they said, easy to apply, long lasting, and unspillable. Forget the practical reasons, I wanted to feel like Cleopatra, smearing perfumed wax behind my ears.

The rest of the trip back to Paris via the Alps, took us about a week. Still camping, and very much in need of a shower, we were thrilled to find that a camp ground outside Grenoble was equipped with showers. So eager, there I was at 7 AM, at 3,000 ft. altitude, trying not to scream as ice-cold water poured down my back. Hearty stock, these mountain climbers. Next time I'll ask if they have <u>hot</u> showers before I rush in.

Completely exhausted, not from the pace, just from trying to absorb so much astonishment, we returned to Paris.

Cold and Tired, Having a Wonderful Time,
C&B

The string bag

10

Paris Again

If April in Paris is grand, surge of background music please, well June is even better. Much warmer, with the big, fat chestnut tree leaves shading all the streets, along with whatever it is that is always "dans l'air" in Paris.

Only one thing has kept us from glorying with each breath we take. When we arrived in Paris last week, in the late afternoon, we went straight to Madame Sordet's Hotel de l'Esperance. But as usual, all the rooms were in use. However, Madame would agree to let us have one "by the whole night" provided we weren't going to stay in Paris too long. We must understand that it was a bit of a sacrifice to rent the room to us that way since she made so much more by the hour. We thanked her for her consideration, said we would be back at 10 o'clock, and promised not to prolong our stay in Paris.

Then we went to see Dean Spille, our old friend from UCLA's Animation Class, whose apartment is in the Place de L'Odeon. We parked right in front of the Opera Comique, and were thrilled to see at least 50 Gendarmes standing at attention in front, their red and blue capes flapping in the breeze. Apparently there was some Gala that evening, and it all looked very impressive.

We had dinner with Dean, and when we returned to our car around 9:30, we noticed the front window had been forced open. A quick check assured us that our cameras, as well as the bag with all our film, exposed and unexposed, had been taken.

In front of 50 policemen?

They were still there, more or less at attention, but could give us no more help than to direct us to the local Commisaire, where we could fill out a report.

So we've spent the last few days filling out police forms checking Lost and Found, filing for insurance, and being terribly depressed, not over the loss of the cameras, since they're insured, nor the unexposed film, but all those marvelous photos we had taken those first exciting days in Paris, as well as the trip south, the Film Festival, and Villa Sans Souci, (I was hoping to <u>show</u> you how Phyllis looks in a bikini), and the Alps.

Worse yet, we realized that our address book was in the stolen bag. Now we lie awake nights trying to remember names and addresses of everyone back home. We keep a pad and pencil by the bed, and each of us wakes up at least once during the night, with some strange recall to put down a name and number. Then it takes us half the morning to try to decipher the chicken scratches.

We've pushed ourselves to get out and try to see more of Paris during those few hours we are free from the bureaucracy of the police and Lost & Found, but things have changed greatly in the month we have been gone. Tourists are piling in at a frightening rate, wandering the streets at large, crowding up the mail counters at American Express. We were here <u>first</u>, darnit!

Meanwhile, through friends, Bob was invited to an animation studio here and they wanted to know if he would consider doing the titles for the new Brigitte Bardot film. What a dilemma! We wanted to continue traveling, we've really hardly started, and if we keep on now while the weather is good we can camp and make our money last much longer. Did I mention that we've kept close accounts and spent $350 the first month, including our "heavy losses" at the Casino? Only $50 over budget. On the other hand, try to think of how Bob will feel giving up the chance to meet Brigitte Bardot?

One other thing: we went to an Artist's Ball in Montparnasse last Saturday night. We had no more walked in when a guy wearing a pair of undershorts and a tuxedo jacket, with tails, started dancing, and what with the lively sort of music they had, it wasn't very long before his private parts were bob-bobbing around in time to the music. Then he got bored and shucked off the shorts altogether, leaving him in the altogether, at least from the waist down.

As the evening wore on, he and his friends, who were wearing wild blue leotards and pink striped shirts, played their instruments, musical and otherwise, upsetting the real band no end, and complaining bitterly, as they came up to me to say that this wasn't a real artists' ball, because if it were, people would be having sex all over the floor instead of wasting their time dancing.

I nodded sympathetically, mumbling my standard "C'est la vie" with the best accent I could muster, which wasn't too great under the circumstances.

Then around one or two in the morning they had a contest for the best model in Montparnasse. Nude, gorgeous, beautiful girls. Poor Bob. I'm enclosing a photo of him showing the effects of France and French women. By the way, the photo also demonstrates the inherent dangers of getting a hair-cut in foreign climes. Bob didn't know how to say "stop" in French, and now German people in the street rush up to him to ask the time and directions. He also caught a cold from the drafts rushing about his head. At least, budget wise, we're in better shape: He won't need another hair cut until late Autumn, at best.

We left Montparnasse around 3 AM and things were still going, going, going...

I'll also enclose a label-you probably wouldn't believe me on this either-of the French equivalent to Coke. It's called Pschitt, pronounced just the way you think, 'Ask For It By Name!' It's just fair tasting, but we keep ordering it just for the fun of it.

Note: As far as we can tell, there are only two ice-cooled drinking fountains in all of Paris, one at the American Embassy, and the other at American Express, which also has a Coke (not Pschitt) machine.

Not Homesick,
C&B

Joan Miro Mural
Postcard

Thought you'd enjoy this postcard view of Joan Miro's UNESCO mural, "The Wall of the Moon". Great building, the murals and sculpture are beautiful, and the Noguchi Japanese garden is just marvelous. We went to the restaurant on the top floor, and watched the sun set over the Eiffel Tower, with Sacre Coeur in the background. Then during a delicious dinner with excellent wine (all in the budget), we saw the lights come on all over Paris. "A Good Moment". The following night we walked to the Seine by Notre Dame, and at 10 o'clock sharp, Handel's Fire

and Water music came out of an elaborate loud-speaker system, as small boats pulled up and began spraying huge jets of water over the river, through changing colored lights, while another fantastic display of fireworks filled the sky behind Notre Dame! I'm getting pretty good at tight-squeeze postcard writing, aren't I? The only thing I haven't taken into consideration is whether anyone can read what I've written.

C&B

11

North by Northeast

We finally gave up trying to recover bag, film, exposed and unexposed, address book, and cameras. It was definitely a case of Hoping Against Hope. We phoned the studio to ask about the Brigitte Bardot film. They said to "keep in touch, things may start around July 1st."

We've received lots of postcards from some of our Maasdam friends who have pin-ball machined their way through six or seven countries already and are practically ready to go back home. We began to feel guilty, since we hadn't even "Done" France yet. I doubt if we'll ever catch up with them (do we want to?).

All of the above made us decide to give up lunches at La Coupole, afternoon strolls in Montparnasse, dinners with new friends, late evening coffee at Deux Maggots...the Louvre, Jeu de Paumes...and move on.

Saying au revoir to all the friends we had met, especially Mme. Sordet was not easy. We have become very chers amis. We were, after all, allowed to stay chez her hotel for over two weeks. She even invited us to aperitifs one evening, with two of her close friends. I think part of our charm is that we're involved with films. She loves the cinema, and we have spent long and arduous hours trying to discuss movie stars in French. This was a bit of a struggle, to say the least, because my morning Adult French Extension Class last winter did not really leave me completely fluent. (Can you believe I got to UCLA every morning at 8 AM? And to The Herman Miller Furniture Company office in Venice by 9:20? And wasn't that nice of them to let me make up the time in the afternoon?)

Bob, who made no such effort or sacrifice, and who did nothing more than look over my shoulder occasionally as I sat pouring over my homework every night and repeat such useful phrases as "Jacques sonne a la porte. La bonne ouvre", ("Jack sounds at the door. The maid opens."), and joke about "My aunt lives in the inkwell", now carries on rather decently in French while I fret over whether the adjective is agreeing with the noun and which tense to try to conjugate. By the time I do decide, the sentence, to say nothing of the entire conversation has moved on and I've lost track and the meaning of both.

Actually our conversations with Mme. Sordet were a rather arcane form of Charades. For example, she loves Catreenaybern. Got it? Katerine Hepburn. We got hints, of course, like "She won the ohscaire." Zchanz/zhay/row/zhay is most definitely Ginger Rogers. Animated films? Deesnay, what else? One night we even branched into jazz and talked about the great DuklingTONE.

We left on such good terms she told us to let her know when we would be back in Paris. She would "hold a room for us!", and we were to go straight there to leave all our bags "so they wouldn't be stolen." How about that?! Sure glad we're so proficient at Charades.

On June 16th we got another one of our normal late afternoon starts. We drove northeast for an hour or so when we started passing field after field covered with World War I white crosses. We stopped for the night in Chateau-Thierry, (less than 100 kilometers from Paris, but at least we were on the road again), and camped in another empty, deserted campground. It's colder up here and the French camping season doesn't seem to start until the middle of July. We put up the new tent we bought in Paris, and felt as if we were spending the night with thousands of ghosts.

The following day we drove through a beautiful countryside full of vineyards, to Rheims. CHAMPAGNE! (and Cathedral) It's dispensed here like Pschitt at 25 cents a glass. We visited a cave or two to watch the bottling and corking process; it's still a hand-done operation, from start to finish. A sweet old man who looked as if he were born in the caves and would surely die there, took us deep down into the earth to show us how they turn the bottles, also by hand. You wouldn't want any rough, old machine getting hold of all those bottled bubbles. After seeing such tender, loving care, I won't complain too much about the price of Piper Heidseck anymore.

We detoured to see friends of friends at the U.S. Air Force Base in Nancy. At the PX, we could hardly believe our eyes. With probably the best bread in the world at the corner bakery just down the street, they air-lift planeloads of packaged white blah loaf bread from the States.

A small gathering of the Base people was arranged for our benefit, and we looked forward to spending an evening with the American military folk. However, we found it somewhat difficult to communicate. Bob asked one lieutenant what he did, and he replied, "SCDs, MG 4-5s, XKYs, you name it!" which ended that conversational tack. I countered to his wife nearby with "Have you been able to travel much?" "Oh, yes," she answered enthusiastically...

"We've just come back from the PX over in Germany somewhere, and every chance we get we check out PX's all over the place." From that point it was all downhill, and we left rather early to wend our way back to the campground in Europe.

Yesterday we drove from Nancy and stopped in Luxembourg for lunch at an Inn beside a river full of trout. "Notre Specialite: Les Truits" What else would it be? And what else would we order?

When the waiter appeared, and spoke English, we were both surprised and grateful, it had been such a struggle the past weeks in France. It had also been a problem trying to avoid wine with our breakfast everyday just because our breakfast hour happened to coincide with French lunch time, which other than the wine problem worked out rather well since that was the only way we were ever going to get an omelette instead of just rolls and coffee for breakfast. But try as we would we could never convince them to bring us, not wine, but coffee, with our eggs. So when our English-speaking waiter in Luxembourg asked us what we were going to drink with our trout, I said, not daring to push our luck and ask for coffee, but hoping for a brief respite from all the wine we've been drinking, "I'll wait". Bob said, "I'll wait too". The waiter marked his pad saying, "Yes sir, two Waits", and off he went.

Panic. What was a "Wait" and how much could it cost? We sat and squirmed, thinking mainly of our budget, until the trout arrived with two glasses of *white* wine. What a relief. We drank it gratefully and even asked for more: "Two more 'Waits' please!"

We spent the afternoon driving to Belgium. Imagine! Three countries in one afternoon. We stopped at the "4 Rois: Café-Hotel-Restaurant-Tea-Room-Pension," (what have they missed, Conference Hall?) for our first dinner in Belgium, and dined on the terrace under a warm, kind of electric summer sky.

Then drove through miles of lush forest which continued to the actual city limits of Brussels. Surely the most beautiful approach into a city we've ever seen. Where were the low-rent districts? Where were the factories?

Bigger surprise: a main square which comes very close to beating out Times Square for amount of neon per square yard or meter as the case may be. Very sophisticated, busy city.

We're camped outside the center and may stay on for several days. Everyone we've met has been extraordinarily helpful and very, very pleasant. The owner of the campground, "Just call me 'Maurice'" speaks seventeen or eighteen languages, he says he keeps losing count. He bounds around with endless energy and good-will, and has promised to knock on our tent (how does one do that?) at 4 AM tomorrow morning and take us with him to the market place set up in the old main square, which has been in constant and uninterrupted service since the 12th or 14th century, give or take a century, when the farmers received the right from the Crown. Progress and civilization, namely automobiles, are crowding them out. The space is needed for parking, and they must clear out by 8 or 9 each morning.

Day's Later:

We did it! I did it! Rose in time to go see the market. It was all quite beautiful and unreal, but then anything would be unreal to me at that hour. The thing I remember most is coming back to our tent with our string bags full for a feast of king-size strawberries, and bananas with yogurt, fresh scrambled eggs with smoked ham, sweet rolls and coffee, made on our 1-burner GAZ stove. Somehow going out to get your provisions at that hour makes one feel more worthy of them-the same way I felt eating the radishes we grew in my first grade playground.

Aside: It's really funny to see Del Monte products in the "Exotic Food" sections in the grocery stores.

We went out to see last year's World Fair grounds. A modern ghost city. We went up into the Atomium, wandered through the empty tubes, up escalators which are no longer working, finally had coffee in the emptied out restaurant on top. I think they will leave the Atomium, but are leveling away everything else. Very strange wandering around all that windswept space.

Schedule Schmedule! Stayed over a week in Brussels, mainly because we were waiting for the tent to dry out-it never seems to stop raining in Europe. At this rate it will take us years to see Europe.

We saw Waterloo, drove through the Flemish countryside, saw our very first windmill, and canals, and handmade lace curtains in all the windows. We actually passed lovely old ladies in what looked like costumes to us, but were obviously their everyday dresses, sitting in the sun making lace. It is an intricate, difficult art, one which is rapidly dying out since none of the young girls want to sit in the sun and make lace all day. No wonder, but too bad.

We also took a boat trip down the canals and saw old Flemish castles and houses along the banks. Lovely, wonderful, fantastic. I've just got to find more and better adjectives. Right now my head feels like a big funnel, filling up with sights and impressions, much more than can sink in through the narrow opening, to be processed and absorbed, alas.

Dazzled,
C&B

American Express Travelers Cheque reciept

12

Amsterdam

A photographer popped up just as we were stepping into this boat which tours the canals in Amsterdam. An hour later on our way out he sold us this "postcard". They should print the following blurb: "One of the native population's most popular pastimes is watching all the eager tourists arrive and depart on these colorful boats"

We're tromping all over dikes, up and down windmills, across the Zuider Zee. Hello Hans Brinker! Big news is that we decided to splurge on a hotel. Bob heard they did big breakfasts in Holland, included in price of the room. True: soft-boiled eggs, a platter of cold, sliced roast-beef, another platter of sliced edam cheese, a basket of fresh bread, rolls and ruskets, pots of honey and jam, lots of luscious butter, pitchers of hot coffee with jugs of thick cream. They should charge for the breakfast and give the room free.

I was mainly interested in a real bathroom... (did I mention that one used buckets to flush the toilets in the campground in Brussels? Notices in many languages tacked on the walls instruct users to empty bucket, then please refill it at the pump outside and replace it full for the next user. I could hardly believe you don't really need a flush, the water goes down by some sort of gravity or magic. Amazing how uninformed we city folk are. Sometimes I cheated, and refilled the bucket twice just to watch the water go down by itself. One must learn to enjoy the simple things in life like non-flush toilets in campgrounds in Belgium) ... I was beginning to look very European with hairy legs and armpits to match. (How they make fun of us American, clean-shaven girls.)

So we're in a "nice, clean, modest" (read inexpensive), hotel on a tree-lined canal. How could we miss, there are over 80 canals in Amsterdam? But the most important thing to us is that Anne Frank's house is on the same street. They are restoring it, planning to turn it into a youth hostel. I'm full of feelings about her and Amsterdam, but can't squeeze more onto this postcard. Will write from Sweden where we intend to stop and regroup forces.

C&B

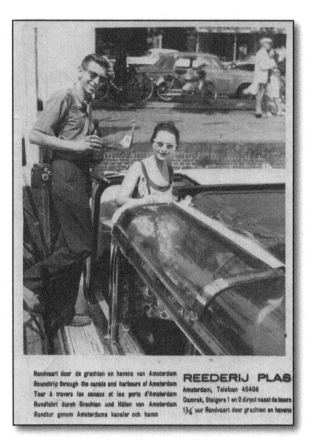

Rondvaart door de grachten en havens van Amsterdam
Roundtrip through the canals and harbours of Amsterdam
Tour à travers les canaux et les ports d'Amsterdam
Rundfahrt durch Grachten und Häfen von Amsterdam
Rundtur genom Amsterdams kanaler och hamn

REEDERIJ PLAS
Amsterdam, Telefoon 45406
Damrak, Steigers 1 en 2 direct naast de beurs
1¾ uur Rondvaart door grachten en havens

Photo of Bob and Cima on boat on canal tour

13

Dutch Aerogramme

I suppose "NIETS INSLUITEN" means "No Enclosures", but it sounds more formidable in Dutch. The rest of it: "Indien Zulka toch geshiedt, dan wordt deze brief per boot/trein ver zonden" you figure out…

We stayed in the GRAND HOTEL FRIGGE" in Gronigen, visited WYNAND FOCKINK; "Opposite the Royal Palace, WYNAND FOCKINK'S original 17th century tasting room. You will enjoy sampling the famous liqueurs and gin in this quaint and friendly atmosphere." Not as much as just saying it – fortunately it tastes pretty good since we order it every time we can.

Holland has the best road and street signs of all. Since streets in Europe were built long before automobile traffic, and consequently have had to be "routed" to handle modern traffic situations, there is at least one sign on every street prohibiting entry to some kind of vehicle. The universal "prohibit" sign is round, white, with a red circle around the border. Whatever is prohibited is pictured in the middle with a red diagonal line across it from border to border. Seeing one of these signs with an auto in the middle means that cars must not enter or travel on that street.

But in Holland there are strings of circle signs with horse-drawn carts, carts pulled by hand; cows, horses, pigs.

One other thing: many buildings with windows on the street side, are equipped with double mirrors, one on each side, so that occupants can sit and watch everything happening below. I hope T.V. doesn't replace this as a national pastime.

I shouldn't have made paragraphs, now I don't have room for a signature.

14

Hamburg Postcard

Thought you'd enjoy this postcard (another Freebee) of the "Bikini Jungmuhle Galopp Diele" in Hamburg on the Riepersbahn, of course. This is where the girls wrestle with each other in the mud. "Damem en schlamen". "Girls" as in 40year old matrons with whom I would hate to wrestle, in or out of the mud. One nudge with their biceps and I'd be flattened. Forget about the glamour also, besides their 200 lb. frames, they wear tight rubber bathing caps, with their ears poking out. The Germans sure have some funny ideas about sex. Anyhow, we're here having your anniversary present drink which is the first such we've had splashed with mud...and enjoying the whole spectacle, not the least interesting being the band which is a regular Rogue's Gallery. I almost expect the bass player to pull out a gun instead of his bow. Gotta go they have phones on each table and someone is calling Bob. As long as it's one of the performers I don't have to worry, but you never can tell.

C&B

15

Big Postcard from Hamburg

We almost stopped traffic in Hamburg-well, in a building. They have the most weird open-faced elevators, big, three-sided boxes on a conveyor system, and as we later found out, one is supposed to jump on and off at the floor of your choice. Dumb Americans, we took one look and said, "You could get killed".

So we pushed the 'stop' button so we could get on safely. Stop it did, right between floors. All we could see were half-bodies up and half-bodies down. Then the screaming started. People came rushing from all over, yelling at us and waving their arms, as the bodies with heads in one elevator box shook their fists at us, while the ones in the box above leaned over so we could <u>see</u> their angry faces. What a scene!

Finally, the janitor limped over, (all janitors seem to limp in Germany), pushed another button, and it all started moving again, and we jumped onto what had really be-come a moving monster. It wasn't easy seeing all the open floors flying past, nor trying to remember what floor it was we wanted to jump off at, because all I could think of was what would happen when we got to the top? Would we be turned upside down on the other side or what? And what if some other dumb tourist pushed the button just as we were stepping off? Maybe that's why so many janitors in Germany limp?

More Language Lessons: In these northern parts, "fahrt" means "trip". "Infahrt" or variations thereof, means "Entrance". "Outfahrt", and variations, "Exit", and "Rundfahrt", "Round Trip". Seems we've been fahrting all over the place. I wish Bob would quit calling me Fahrt Fuhrer.

Ever on the move, especially in elevators,
C&B

16

North by North

Here I sit, in a tiny "sun-room", on the 6th or 7th floor, they're sneaky, you never can tell in Europe. They don't count the first floor, that's "Ground Floor". The one above that is "lst Mezzanine" followed by "2nd Mezzanine", then "3/4 Mezzanine", (honestly), and finally the lst Floor. Maybe. In Copenhagen we were offered a room which they had the nerve to tell us was on the 4th floor, explaining that there wasn't any elevator. We took it, figuring 4th floor up couldn't be so bad. There were 150 steps by our count, and starting at ground level, 7 floors.

When we tried to buy pillows in a large department store in Rotterdam, the girl at the Information Desk told us we would find bed supplies "on the 3rd floor, 4th for Americans..."

Anyhow, here I am, in our hotel room in Stockholm, it's pouring down rain, the chimes are ringing all over town for the Sondag (Sunday) church services, and we're going to Moscow on Tisday (Tuesday).

But I digress.

I'm sorry I haven't written anything but postcards for so long, but when we're constantly on the road, it's hard to get to the typewriter which lives in the far corner of the trunk, under the air mattresses and Klompen (wooden shoes,) and I'm too embarrassed to tell you about those.

Now I'll begin with our driving into Bruges in the rain (as I said, it really rains a lot in Europe, which among other things, plays havoc with my naturally curly hair), parking in the main square and sitting there in the car looking through the sploshed windshield at the beautiful banners-red-and-black-lions on a gold background-flying from the old medieval buildings, and listening to the carillon in the bell-tower which was built before Columbus discovered America.

Later we climbed all 350 steps of the bell tower-they announce the total as you reach the top. Once we recovered and adjusted to the thin air and whistle of the wind we looked out over the red tile rooftops to see the beautiful Belgian landscape spread out in all its glory and again I realized that those Flemish painters didn't invent a thing. From what we could see, not too much has changed since then either, landscape-wise.

One of the two men who play what is reputed to be the finest carillon in the world, personally showed us the 47-bell keyboard, and told us how he has played them every-day for 26 years. "A job's a job-no difference if I worked in a factory, or climb these stairs six times a day to wind the clock and play the bells...only thing is they've asked me to go to New York next September, to play a carillon they've got there...not as old or fine as this, of course, but I'd still like to go, been here all my life, and it would be nice to see another part of the world before I die." On the way down we noticed names scratched on the walls. One read "Henrik Van Flyden 1285".

Bruges at night: they illuminate the canals with soft

yellow, blue, and white lights. The willow trees branch down into the water, and the swans glide quietly by. Much too much like a fairy-tale for comfort.

As if all this weren't enough, there is a small museum here, just large enough to hold several masterpieces of Flemish painting, only one in each room. Truly thrilling. Curators of the world, please note.

On to Holland, via Breskens and the ferry to Middleburg. The first night we camped in a field outside of town next to a canal and windmill. The next morning we tried out the wooden shoes, which are a bit clumsy but pretty practical for tromping around all that water. By the way we were very careful to buy plain klompen, nothing with "Souvenir of Holland" painted garishly on each shoe. Then we saw most of the farmers wearing the painted, not plain, variety. There's a message there somewhere, but I'm not quite sure what it is.

Next morning we went to the noted Work-Horses Market in Middleburg, and all I can say is those horses looked about as much like the horses we know as a lion does a cat. They were short with enormous-huge, thick legs, and beautiful, heavy manes in back of large, full heads. Built for hard work, not speed.

Rotterdam is impressive. The city was leveled by the Germans, but the people we talked to feel they must forget. They say there is a whole new generation which didn't participate in the war and, after all, business is business. However, they do resent the fact that somehow Germany is now the wealthiest country in Europe.

Forced to rebuild their city, they could indulge in creative city planning, with a master plan, and consistency of architecture. The result is very exciting, with dramatic uses of steel, glass, and all the modern materials and methods now available. We saw a restaurant being constructed on the ground, later to be hoisted to the top of a 120 ft. high column.

There is great extravagance in the exterior decorations-mosaics, brick bas relief, steel and concrete sculpture. But the truly wonderful thing is that with all this outburst of contemporary architecture and design, there are still lace curtains on many of the windows of these steel and glass buildings.

They have a large shopping "street" for pedestrians only-no cars (or carts), repeat NO CARS. They have automats in the streets dispensing fresh flowers. Nice to know you can buy a fresh rose at 3 in the morning. A bakery shop had a display of flower arrangements all made of chocolate, including the vase. One shoe store window was filled with sea shells. Parrots were wandering around free and easy.

We bought two pillows and two pillowcases, which took most of one afternoon, but it was sheer heaven camping that night, especially since there was a violent wind that almost blew the car away, but we could bury our heads in our new pillows. Now that I think of it, however, that was the night we forgot to buy water and had to take our vitamins with B & B, so with or without pillows, maybe that's why, in spite of the wind, we slept so well.

Some nights we also take our vitamins with our now favorite popular Dutch liqueur Wynand Focking. Yes, we bought it for its name, then found out it's really good, and definitely another fast way to get to sleep.

The next morning, we washed up in the farmer's milk shed, and he invited us in for a cup of Droste's hot chocolate. We told him that Bob's grandmother had always served it to him when he was a boy, with a glob of fresh butter, but I don't think he thought much of the idea, or really cared that Drostes was popular in Rochester 30 years ago.

Den Haag next, then Amsterdam, with yet more canals and even more bicycles. Holland is a bike-per-person country. They have an extra lane on all the highways just to handle bike traffic. Before we realized this, we stopped along the road for our usual picnic lunch. We were looking forward to all kinds of herring, cheese, and fresh everything else, tomatoes, fruit, bread, and were delighted to find this nice wide space alongside the main road. We pulled over, parked, set up our camp table and chairs, spread out our feast, and were about to try to go native and eat our herring by holding it up with our right hand and popping it into our open mouths, when we saw several bikes coming our way. They stopped and tried to pass us politely. No explanations. When that happened a dozen more times in the next ten minutes we began to realize that something was amiss, namely us. Right. We were in the middle of the bike-not path-but a full, wide paved road, like I said, adjacent to the main road. Beyond embarrassed, we gulped down the rest of our lunch, and very hurriedly got out of the way of noon bike traffic.

In the cities, bikes have the right of way, as well they should, there are a lot more of them than us in automobiles. It took us the longest time to figure out what the long, diagonal slots in the streets in Rotterdam were for: Bike Parking Places. And we never cease to enjoy the sights we see on bikes-people walk their dogs on bikes; teenagers ride along holding hands, a boy reaches across to keep a hand on his girl's waist.

As for canals, they are now giving lessons to the people on how to get out of a car which has fallen into a canal. Apparently the rate of cars falling into canals and consequent drowning is such that they are in need of a mass education program. Fact: it costs $10 to pull your car out of a canal.

We looked up the local representative of Herman Miller Furniture Co., a very nice rosy-cheeked Dutchman, Herr Bakker, and he spent several days with us rounding up Herman Miller chairs and then helping us cart them all over the countryside until we found a green grassy field with a pretty windmill standing in the middle, in front of which we could photograph the chairs. Lots easier than trying to shoot HM tables in front of the Eiffel Tower. In fact, we got so discouraged in France that we almost wished we hadn't promised the Herman Miller Advertising Department that we would take picturesque photos of their furniture all over Europe.

It was dear Herr Bakker who pointed out the ubiquitous hooks extending out of every gable, and explained that the only way most furniture could be moved into any old building was through the windows, hence the permanent hooks, over which a cable system allows anything bigger than a campstool to be yanked up with rope and pulley.

He took us to a cheese factory where we learned how to open and serve Edam and Gouda properly. No hacking it in segments. One scores and removes a neat, small circle in the top. Then one can either scoop, or continue to score bigger circles and wedges from the top down. Very neat and tidy, and oh, what a difference it is to eat fresh cheese, no matter how you cut it. We bought one of each for the road. Too bad we couldn't do the same when we visited the diamond cutters.

Of course, we spent most of our days in the famous museums, but one night we looked for a different cultural experience and visited the equally famous Seamen's

District. Bob especially was very impressed. Block after block of women, all different types, from skinny-prissy to fat-bosomy, perched in their front windows, under a red light, For Rent. The whole idea is to window-shop, literally. Some women sit there reading thick books, others toy with a whip, some look bored, others almost reach out and grab.

When the decision is made, the lady comes down out of her window, lets you in, and pulls the drape shut. When she is ready for the next customer, she opens the curtain, takes her place in the window and resumes her pose. For those of you who are interested in the economics of the situation, the current market price per stuckt is 10 guilders, or roughly $2.50.

Another night we decided to go to a movie. Well, we hadn't seen a film since Paris and we needed a fix. We found something that looked interesting, "Bad Man From Montana", and went up to the box office around 8 o'clock. They wouldn't sell us a ticket, and we couldn't understand what they were trying to tell us. Finally the woman in the box-office and the usher got so frustrated, they sold us two tickets and showed us in.

The movie ended 30 minutes later, the lights went on and everyone, mostly men, got up and left. The usher came over to us, started talking again, and motioning, and pointing to his watch, and we still didn't know what the problem was. Then the cleaning crew came in. By now we were very chummy with the usher, who again made signs and motioned that we were fine where we were, not to bother ourselves. We had had no intention of moving, as the ladies mopped and swept around us.

Finally, a new crowd came in all at once and sat down. Fifteen minutes later the lights dimmed. News, cartoons, coming attractions, lots of commercials, then INTERMISSION.

As I recall, it was 10 PM when "Bad Man From Montana" actually hit the screen again and by the time it came to the part where we had come in originally, we began to get the message, and stayed in our seats to the end. Apparently there are special show times, and one doesn't just wander in and out at any old time. No wonder they didn't know what to do with us, and weren't they nice to a couple of greenhorns?

Our hotel was on the same street as Anne Frank's house. We were told that Amsterdam misses its Jews, that they provided wit and charm. All the old comedians came from "The Quarter" and for some reason can't seem to be replaced. The few Jews now remaining have erected a statue of a Dutch dockworker, in the middle of the old Quarter. This is in memory of the dock workers who went on strike when the Germans started taking away the Jews, apparently tying up things so badly that the Germans were forced to relent somewhat, and things went a bit easier for the Jews, at least briefly.

The King of Belgium paid a state visit to Queen Juliana while we were there. We followed the parade to the palace, and stood along the canals and waved to the King and Queen as they cruised through the city. Why can't we have a king and queen like all these lucky Europeans? They have all the fun. Palaces, guards, flags, banners, parades, tea parties...princes, princesses, diamonds, jewels, tiaras, and crowns...

As we were leaving Holland we went across the sea wall, 18 miles of man-made island blocking off the North Sea and forming the Zuider See. I can't tell you how impressive it is to be in Holland, and to realize that although it looks like other countries, it is built on land which is 10 to 30 feet below sea level. In Holland you don't just see dikes, you're *on* them most of the time. It is also amazing to see with what nonchalance they have managed to overcome overwhelming obstacles. When we asked someone how they managed to build a dike 18 miles long in the middle of the ocean, he answered, "Oh, just by pouring things in, you know-buckets and truckloads of rock, sand, and debris, until eventually it reaches the top".

Another thing: "So it shouldn't be a total loss," on this dike to beat all dikes, along the sides of the road they use the "extra" two or three feet to graze sheep!

It was on a Sunday that we crossed the border to Germany. In Holland, people were slowly promenading, riding bicycles, all rather peaceful. Not in Germany. Achtung! Physical Activity everywhere: swimming, boating, hiking, running, riding, all at a terrific pace. Exhausting just to watch, let alone do.

We stopped for a quick lunch: herring sandwich and a long sausage poking out of a small round roll. I couldn't figure out if you were supposed to eat the roll, or if was just cheaper than a napkin and only meant to hold the sausage so that you would keep your fingers clean.

Even so my hands got dirty and I went to a public underground rest room to wash them. It cost 30 phennings. There was a very detailed chart outlining all the charges for use of toilet: with or without toilet paper, hand washing, with or without soap/towel. I didn't have any deutsche marks yet and left to get some change from Bob. The large, German lady attendant chased me up the stairs, out and across the street, screaming as she ran. By the time I noticed her, traffic had stopped on both sides of the road. For 30 phennings? I'm sure glad I didn't run up a bigger bill, might have been hauled in on heaven only knows what charge. ("She used two squares of toilet paper and only paid for one!")

We finally got to Hamburg and American Express to pick up our mail. Panic. There was a letter from Cineaste offering Bob the job in Paris. Immediately. Fortunately, their offer was so low we honestly couldn't afford to take it. We would be spending some of own money, and even Brigitte Bardot isn't worth that. We wrote them giving our minimum, and went off to Denmark with pure hearts.

Then when we got to Copenhagen, we found a wire from Cineaste, "Job yours return as quickly as possible". We were sick! We couldn't turn down so much money and also louse up chances to work there later, but we weren't at all ready to settle down yet. We sweated for four hours before I noticed the date on the telegram. It had been sent last month! They must have sent it before they received our letter telling them we were stopping in Hamburg. What a relief...

We caught up with some Maasdam friends in Copenhagen and spent a very pleasant afternoon comparing notes and museum-dropping..."Didn't you go to the museum in Grenoble? Fabulous!" They are all buying Danish furniture like crazy here and planning on catching the August 4th ship back to New York, while we feel we're just really getting started.

Aside: We saw a blind beggar with a phonograph in his lap, playing records. He couldn't play an instrument, apparently, but did wind a mean phono. We gave him 50 ore for effort.

Driving in the countryside we passed a crumbling wall, Bob stopped the car, rushed over to it and finally got his chance to say, "Something is rotten in the state of Denmark". I try not to encourage this sort of thing, but obviously I'm not always successful.

We stayed in a private home in Copenhagen. They have a fine system whereby private homes are made available to tourists for a nominal fee. That way one can see how people live, make friends, and at the same time help them earn extra money.

Our hostess, Fru Fisher, is German born. After her French mother died, when Fru Fisher was four, she moved to Russia with her father. They lived there until the first World War, then returned to Germany, where she eventually married a Dane, and has been in Copenhagen ever since. Her artist husband (the apartment is filled with his German Expressionist paintings) died four years ago. There were no children and she was left with this large apartment, so she rents out the extra rooms, and in this way satisfies her abundant maternal instincts and budget problems at the same time.

We had a wonderful room with a brass-frame bed and down comforters, (appropriately called "Dooners"). Heaven. Fru Fisher tip-toed around in the morning, trying not to disturb our sleep, so slobs that we are, we slept until noon, staggered out of bed and into the dining-room where she prepared a sumptuous breakfast for us: soft-boiled eggs, really soft and really hot, unlike the cold, hard-boiled variety we've almost, but not completely gotten used to, cheese, assorted breads, slabs of fresh butter, home made marmalade (she gave me the recipe, but unless I have a month or two to dedicate to nothing but making orange marmalade, I don't think I'll ever get into production), three varieties of honey ("I didn't know if you preferred heather or light,") pots of hot coffee and tea, ("I thought you might want to try both"), with thick, fresh cream. While we were out, she washed and ironed all my blouses, tidied up our things for us, and generally made herself useful. For all of this plus her own charming company, we paid $3.00 a night.

Ah, Tivoli. Do Not think "amusement park". We've never seen anything remotely like it anywhere. It's right in the center of town, with something there for everyone. Small lakes for boating, dance pavilions, a concert hall, pantomime theater, an open-air stage with performances two times a night, no fewer than twenty-one restaurants, all kinds, from plush terrace dining to hot-dog stands, a good size Ferris wheel-roller coaster type area- and a children's playground in which *we* could spend a week or two just looking at the bamboo bird-shaped covered slide, fish swings, huge rooster teeter-totters, mosaic covered forms for climbing, wonderful, wonderful bells to ring, and the trash containers are cement hippos with their mouths wide open to receive all the debris. Oh, and fireworks twice a week. Amazing. Admission is 14 cents, cheaper if you buy a season ticket, and most of the entertainment is free. And that's what people in Copenhagen do from May to September.

By now we had covered a lot of kilometers, and even at our snail's pace, we were tired, not so much physically-most people in the American Express mail lines look gaunt, emaciated, and hollow-eyed, and stare when my chubby little self, with my Dutch milk-maid apple cheeks joins them. They always ask when we had arrived in Europe, and where we have been. I usually try to get away with just answering one question, not the two together. I tried that once and told some exhausted young man that we had arrived the end of April and had already seen parts of France, Luxembourg, and Belgium. He looked at me kind of funny and said, "Not Spain? Italy? Germany? That's all???" So we keep our little secrets.

Anyhow, let's say we were spiritually tired. Yes, that's it. From trying to absorb all that is beautiful, wonderful, different, stimulating, exciting, and just plain fun. So we decided to do what all the rest of these people do in the summer: go to the country. And what better country in which to go to the country? Sweden, of course.

So off we went onto another ferry, but when we got off that ferry, and started to drive into the traffic, OOPS! Lord, we'd forgotten and no one had chosen to remind us that they drive on the left side in Sweden. Bob, with his nonchalant free-form driving skills, is doing rather well. I, as a pedestrian, however, cannot say the same. Look to the right I keep telling myself, forgetting that halfway across the street I've suddenly got to look right <u>and</u> left and around in back for someone making a left-hand turn, which is really a right turn here, get it?

Each new country has its different sounds, and it's wonderful to hear different sounding trains, chimes, and especially, of course, language. Danish is kind of throaty, while Swedish seems to happen right up between the lips.

We got locked in a castle. All visitors had to take the guided tour, and once it got started, we found that the guide only spoke Swedish, which was perfectly fine for the twenty other people, but not for us, so we just walked on ahead, looked into the empty castle rooms, not terribly interesting as castle rooms go, and very cold, and thought it best to leave, only to find that we were locked in. So we sat on the damp stairs seeing the nice hot sun outside, through a crack in the door, and waited while the guide gave a lecture in each of the 40 or so rooms in the Slot. Well, some people were locked in castles for 20 years or more so we didn't feel it was right to complain. But next time we'll be sure to ask for the details, such as possible exits.

Lakes everywhere, all seemingly bordered with willows and reeds. The sun strikes the water in that beautiful, diffused, way we've seen in all those Swedish movies, which explains why these fair-skinned girls get such great tans.

After another dose of rain as we left Denmark, the sun came out. How wonderful it was to spend those days camping in the lake country in central Sweden. There are now 19 hours of daylight here, so that even after watching the ducks on the lake as the sun set around 10:30 and we crawled into our tent, it was still light, and when we got out of the tent the next morning around 7:30, it was bright and clear. We hopped into the cool, quiet, and clear lake, (so clear we could watch small schools of minnow biting our toes) for a pre-breakfast swim, then had coffee and breakfast rolls (which along with their sweet cookies seem to be made with a mild pepper which gives them a nice tang, like that of good, fresh nutmeg) relaxed, and recovered from such a hectic beginning of the morning. Next, in for another swim. If we are moving on that day, we pull up the tent, which takes all of five minutes, and get into the car, still in our suits, so we can plunge into any inviting lake we pass on our way.

So many forests, everything is built of wood, giving the small towns we passed the look of a turn-of-the-century western town. Sort of early San Luis Obispo mixed with late Disneyland. Jonkoping at the tip of Lake Vattern is the "Match Capital of the World", and we have a great souvenir collection of 50 small wooden match boxes to prove it. I know, but we can't help the occasional lapse, and we stored them next to the wooden Klompen from Holland.

Our recovery was complete by the time we reached Stockholm. It is built on fourteen islands, all connected with an impressive collection of bridges. There are great granite hills and wonderful old, green colored copper domed buildings which glitter in the morning and the late evening sun.

Our first stop, as usual, was American Express. We were hoping for a letter from a special travel agency in Paris to whom we had written for specific information on how to get to Russia.

Flashback: In Cannes we heard that the Moscow Film Festival, which would take place some time in August, was officially accredited. So figuring it was worth a try, we wrote to the Festival committee, informing them we were representing UCLA's "Film Quarterly" and were "available" to attend their festival. In Hamburg, we received a letter from the festival! But it was in Russian! What did it say? Were we invited???

What a *hassle* trying to get that letter translated. Squirming with curiosity, we tried to find the Russian Embassy. None in Hamburg, not even a Consulate. We went to the American Embassy, where one of the girls dimly remembered some Russian she had studied once in school. No help. Next, we tried a translation agency: $8.50 to translate it into German, and another $8.50 to translate it from German into English. $17 just for translations? We told them to translate it into German and we'd take it from there.

Back at the American Embassy, when they saw what it said-yes, they did understand German-they asked, rather huffily, why we hadn't told them it was official. "We would have taken it to our Press Bureau!"

At that point, four men spent four hours checking to see if 1) the festival was subversive, and 2) what The Policy was on healthy, young Americans attending. After an entire afternoon of this somewhat shocking folderol, they apologetically told us that they could find nothing subversive about it. Further a Policy, had changed somewhat, so they no longer discourage people from attending "these things".

It was only then we found out that not only had we been officially invited, but that the festival would pay expenses for one of us. The letter recommended we write to a specific Paris travel agency to arrange the trip, which we did, giving the Stockholm American Express office as our address.

So, when there was no reply from Paris. We ran to the Intourist agency here in Stockholm and Good Grief found out the festival would start next Monday. Obviously, we had to make a quick decision. This might have been easy, but our money was beginning to run pretty thin. Even though they were willing to pay expenses for one in Moscow, the trip would cost between $200/$300. Remember, we're trying to make $300 last a month.

We spent a sleepless night, trying to decide if one week in Moscow was worth sacrificing two or three weeks of other travel, and if we spent all our money by the time we got back to Stockholm, what would we do?

But by morning, Saturday, we decided that one doesn't get invited to a Film Festival in Moscow everyday. We'd worry about running out of money when we ran out of money, our usual end-of-trip philosophy, even though Dad had made us promise not to wire him for money this time.

First stop: the Intourist travel agency to leave passports for visas. Next, American Express, to cash a personal check so we could reserve two Deck Class passages on the Tuesday boat to Helsinki. But they needed our passports to cash our check; a harried run back to Intourist before they closed for the weekend. Barely made it in time to get our passports and rush back to American Express. Finally, the post-office to mail our passports via registered mail to the Russian Consulate, hoping we would get them back by Tuesday. A very breathless "Whew."

It all somehow worked out and we boarded the ship to Helsinki on schedule. They had made it seem very romantic, "Northern nights under the stars....". We'll arrive in Helsinki the following morning, have the day to look at all the Alvar Aalto buildings, then leave that night on the train, which takes 24 hours to get to Moscow.

We've also booked me on a package tour, which they patiently explained is simply the cheapest way of getting me there, with daily coupons for my keep. It's all rather complicated, but apparently one must buy tourist vouchers for room and board, and use these instead of currency in Russia. I don't quite understand what this accomplishes for their economic system other than keeping alleged paupers away. Since Bob has an official invitation, he didn't need any. So here am I, with room and meal tickets, as well as a daily tour around Moscow, paid for. I may or may not be able to sneak into Bob's room at night, but Intourist assures me that my arrangement is only a formality, and that I need never go to my own hotel, nor join my tour if I don't want to. None the less I have visions of someone blowing the whistle on me and causing an International Incident.

Now we have to reshuffle, repack, buy an alarm clock, small suitcase, (we're determined to Travel Light to Russia-good title for a book) and a Bolex 8 mm camera to replace the one stolen in Paris, and find a place to store the Peugeot. They say the best garage in Stockholm is the Atom-Bomb Shelter they have built inside one of the hills in the center of the city. We must also wire the festival in Moscow to advise them that we will be a few days late, keep our seats for us.

When next you hear from us...or, "Once behind enemy lines, Gridley, you're on your own..."

Definitely not Coolly,
C&B

P.S. I'm enclosing photo of me and the new Parisian hairdo I splurged on, not in Paris, but in Brussels. Needed some kind of moral uplift after so many soggy days in the tent. You can't see the back, but it pooches up in a complicated, tricky and zippy way. Come to look at it, you can't tell too much about the front either. What a crummy picture.

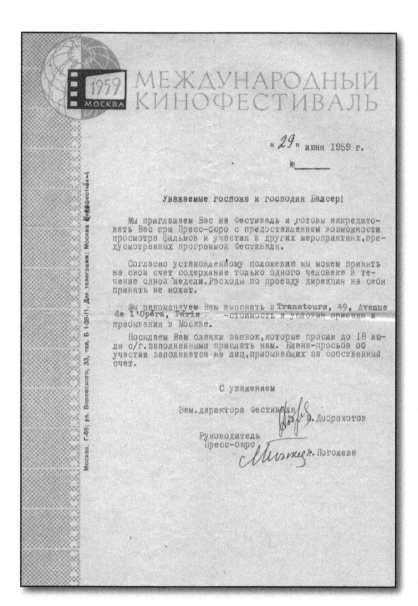

The letter in Russian

The envelope

Moscow Film Festival
Cultural Ministry
Moscow, U.S.S.R.

Attention: Director of Festival, Ju. Dobrochotow
Pressbureau, L. Pogosch'ewa

Gentlemen:

Thank you for your letter inviting us to the Moscow
Film Festival. We are enclosing one of the applications
you sent.

We are now in Hamburg, Germany and are today writing
to Transtours in Paris to make travel arrangements.

We will send you the other application regarding
specific method of transportation and arrival date in
Moscow as soon as we complete our arrangements with
Transtours in Paris.

Thank you again.

Yours sincerely,

Robert and Cima Balser, Film Quarterly
c/o American Express
Paris, France

July 14, 1959

Our letter to the festival

Photo of Cima with new hair do in
front of the Manneken Pis

17

Postcard From Helsinki

Wed. Aug. 5

We left Stockholm noon yesterday in pouring rain. Everyone keeps telling us what a wonderful summer it is here in Europe. We're soaking wet all the time. Just as we were beginning to feel as if we were off on a really strange and exotic adventure the loudspeakers on the ship started playing "Pistol Packin' Mama".

Had lunch, sat on deck watching what seemed like hundreds of islands in the Swedish archipelago go by-and the birds following the ship-and the tugs pulling block-long barges of wood (to the match factory in Jonkoping?), the sun breaking through the clouds in thin rays, blue sky, white clouds, and the loudspeaker finally switched to Beethoven. Then Bob noticed that the charming birds were dropping their droppings on his head.

It was still light long after dinner. Someone brought out an accordion, people started singing and dancing, and I felt just as if we were in the photo on the cover of some travel brochure advertising "Northern Nights Under The Stars". Wow!

Suddenly, as if at some secret signal everyone stopped singing and dancing and just disappeared. All the better for us, we thought, less crowded, as we pulled our deck chairs together, and snuggled in for what we expected to be a peaceful night's sleep. But too soon it got very cold and very damp and I knew I wasn't going to be able to sleep, I turned to see how Bob was and he had disappeared! I jumped up and almost fell over him. He sat up and called out to me, and we started groping for each other. We were both wearing our black raincoats, and had somehow managed to place our deck chairs right under the giant smoke stack which had covered us both in layers of black soot. Black raincoat, black face, he was there beside me all the time.

The worst was yet to come. Freezing, filthy, and with fractured backs, we were forced to go below and soon realized why everyone had been in such a hurry to get inside. There were only a few seats so there were lots of bodies-on the floor, on shelves, curled around and on top of small cocktail tables, most of them snoring. It was hot, there was a terrible pungent odor of damp wool and bare feet, and somehow the lights were still on.

I found a ledge and propped myself up there to doze fitfully until I woke up with one arm asleep, a crick in my neck, and someone's damp smelly stocking feet in my face. It was at that moment, around 3 AM, I decided this should go on record as the longest night in my life, and I prayed for morning to come soon, very soon. So much for "Night Under The Stars."

Now in Helsinki, trying to get my face clean.
C&B

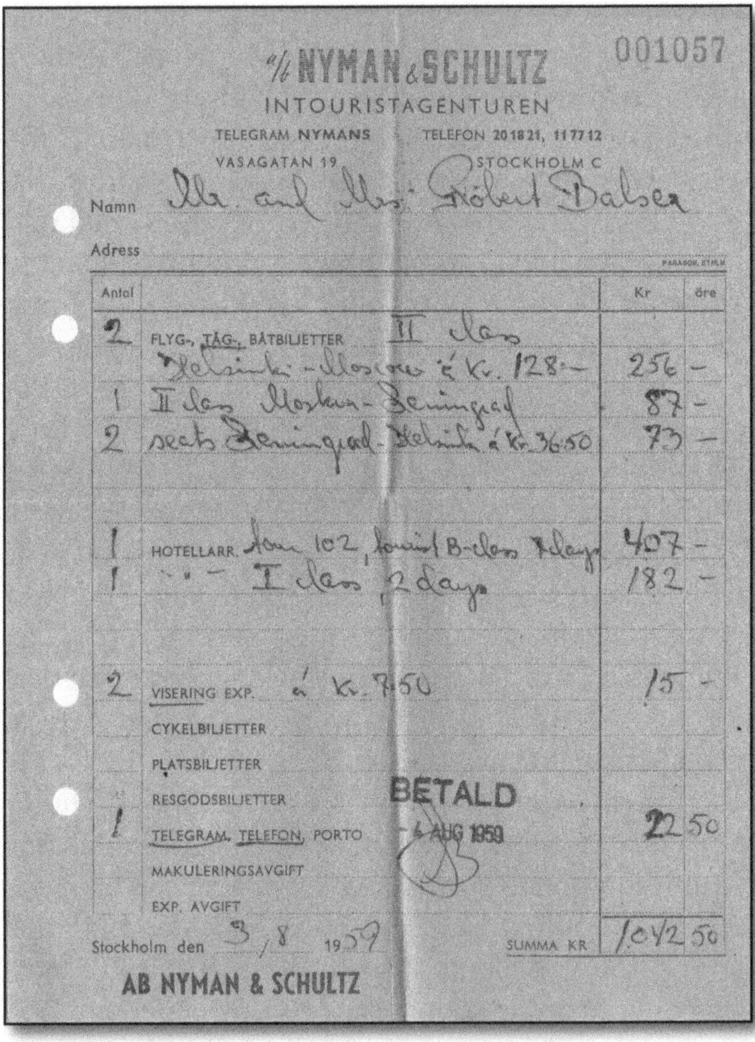

a/b NYMAN & SCHULTZ 001057
INTOURISTAGENTUREN
TELEGRAM NYMANS TELEFON 20 18 21, 11 77 12
VASAGATAN 19 STOCKHOLM C

Namn Mr. and Mrs. Robert Balser
Adress
PARAGON, STHLM

Antal		Kr	öre
2	FLYG-, TÅG-, BÅTBILJETTER II class		
	Helsinki-Moscow à Kr. 128.-	256	-
1	II class Moskva-Leningrad	87	-
2	seats Leningrad-Helsinki à Kr. 36.50	73	-
1	HOTELLARR. Room 102, tourist B-class 7 days	407	-
1	" " I class 2 days	182	-
2	VISERING EXP. à Kr. 7.50	15	-
	CYKELBILJETTER		
	PLATSBILJETTER		
	RESGODSBILJETTER BETALD		
1	TELEGRAM, TELEFON, PORTO 6 AUG 1959	22	50
	MAKULERINGSAVGIFT		
	EXP. AVGIFT		
	Stockholm den 3/8 1959 SUMMA KR	1042	50

AB NYMAN & SCHULTZ

Boat and Train receipt Stockholm Moscow return

18

Russian Diary

Thursday, August 6, 1959

Buy fruit, cookies, bottled water, and postcards at the outdoor market, and board the train to Moscow. All the signs are in Russian. We seem to be the only passengers. Dandelion type puffs fly in the windows and float about through the train, adding to the Doctor Zhivago atmosphere.

We weave our way through several cars and find coach which we think is the dining car, but they only serve "chai" so we have our first Russian tea, served steaming straight from a samovar into glasses in silver holders. The waiter is sweaty, wears an old, soiled, once-white jacket, open to the navel.

On the way back to our seats, and I don't know how, we get locked into a 3rd class compartment, also empty. After much pounding and shouting, a very large woman, wearing a blue beret and bulging out of her skirt, comes to let us out. She yells at us, but we don't know what to answer in response, and head sheepishly back to our seats.

Dirt pours in the windows as we ride through Finland,

leaving layers of grit on everything. I shouldn't have wasted all my soap pads this morning.

Another American comes on board at the border. He's from Oregon and tries to teach us a few Russian words and phrases he has learned. There is plenty of time because the train is stopped for what seems like hours. The customs official and his assistant finally arrive, smiles and very charming but becomes impatient when we don't understand his English. We have to produce our passports, then we're given a declaration to fill out. We must declare all money, jewelry, literature, personal belongings, and fruit. They look through our bags, and finally leave.

Outside on the Russian side there are searchlights and armed guards, and we're beginning to get paranoid, as we suspect there are probably machine guns hidden in the innocuous looking hay stacks in the surrounding fields. The American, Peter, laughs at our suspicions just when we were beginning to enjoy the drama.

We finally move on into Russia. More grit and grime, more chai. We're told there was a dining car, but it was taken off at the border. Still no passengers other than we three Americans.

Pass through countryside for couple of hours before we see a very small station. The train stops, and we think we're told there will be a long delay, so we get out and walk through "town," which is little more than a few unmarked, unpaved, cross streets, several wooden houses, and one grocery. We go in and see caviar displayed in what looks like bedpans. Not too appetizing that way.

As we're walking down the deserted street back to the train I clearly hear, "Ey, Cima!" and turn quickly. Whenever I have heard that throughout my life, I knew whoever was calling was calling me. Well, Grandma said "Cima" was a common Russian name, and someone else here was answering the call. I suppose this goes under the heading of "Finding Your Roots," but it was still a shock.

Beautiful sunset as the train moves on, and we see more people stare at us passing by as we stare at them. There are no cars or traffic of any sort, just people walking. Lots of soldiers. Streets are littered, and torn up in many places. Fashion seems to be Sears-Roebuck catalog, Spring-Summer, 1930. Lots of rayon, loose-fitting dresses, cap-sleeves, faded prints, some must have had belts originally, but they seem to be long gone. Bobby-socks are still in.

The sky lights up and we hang not too far out the window to watch a rather fierce electric storm. We can't hear any thunder, the noise of the train makes it impossible to hear anything else.

We say good-bye to Peter who will get off in Leningrad, and go in to our compartment, take off our shoes, stretch out on the two lower bunks, and fall asleep, telling ourselves yet again, "We really *are* in Russia!"

Sometime in the middle of the night I wake and realize the train has stopped – is it Leningrad? The door of our compartment opens, the light flashes on, I hear voices, then the door closes again.

Thursday, August 6

Morning: When I wake I see a pair of uniformed legs stretching across the bunk above me to the bunk on the other side. These belong to an army officer, who later explains he is only a "Candidate," whatever that means.

He tries to tell us something about arriving at some station, but details, such as when, are rather fuzzy. We offer him some of our provisions which will have to do for breakfast (fruit and cookies), and he waves grandly and manages to get chai all around. He dips his sugar cube into the tea and then bites off the end, just like my grandmother used to do.

We go back to waving out the window and being waved back. The train is finally crowded, and traveling at a good clip. I try to talk to a young girl, around ten years old, standing next to me in the corridor, but we both give up and smile at each other instead.

Our resident army officer, however, continues his efforts at conversation, trying and actually succeeding in telling us he had been in a tanker during the war and visited both the U.S. and Canada. Says he liked it very much, but the Soviet Union is his country, so he must be happy here. He is not Russian, "Ukrainian," has wife and two children, boy and girl. Actually, like most fathers, he is a bit shaky on their exact ages, and works around it by telling us what grades they're in, in school.

He says he is thirty-five. Bob says he is thirty-two. He says they are old men, but Bob contradicts him and says they're young men, after which they arrive at some sort of consensus and agree that since neither one of them likes rock 'n' roll they're "young" but growing "old."

He says Nixon isn't honest, "like Stalin," and using his hand to demonstrate, continues, … "He shows one side of hand to the people, one to the Capitalists, one to the Party." Just as I think he is going to run out of hands, he adds, "Khrushchev is different, he shows same side to everybody. Eisenhower is good general, but not so good President." On that point we shake hands, agreeing and at the same time putting all hands temporarily out of action, hoping to move on to non-political subject.

But he whips out a magazine in which there is an article on the dangers of the new cult of Jehovah's Witnesses, which again takes us to the brink, as he angrily slaps the magazine, we have stopped holding hands by then, and claims that all the J.W. literature comes from the U.S., and why are we exporting this "sickness" to them?

We try to explain that Jehovah's Witness is a very small cult in the U.S., with a very limited appeal, and should not be a big problem in the Soviet Union. Maybe this makes sense to him, or he doesn't understand. He keeps saying "Understand!?" more of a command than a question, or "Understood me?!" He doesn't want us to think he doesn't understand, but for whatever reason he abruptly changes the subject and tries to tell us, with some pride, the people he has seen, "Roosevelt, Eisenhower, Marshall, etc." We hesitate questioning him on this, not wanting to get into the intricacies of the expression "in person" even though we are more than curious, so we back off and ask him for at least the tenth time when he thinks we'll arrive in Moscow. Before he can "understood" we're pulling into the station.

It is 12:30 PM, we leave the train together, stand on the platform taking photos, shaking hands warmly. He gives us a small red and green army button, and we realize we did not come prepared with appropriate gifts to exchange. There is a moment of consternation on our parts until Bob gives him one of his ballpoint pens. We finally say good-bye in both languages, (doughsveedah'nya) along with "Meer Droozhba", which we have learned means "Peace and Friendship." God knows we can all use a lot of that.

We are obviously easy to spot. A man comes up to ask if there are any other tourists on the train. He seems more confused than we, and when we say we don't know but don't think so, he leads us to a car and tells the driver something, for all we know we're on the way to Siberia, but at least it will be an adventurous drive because why should Russian taxi drivers be any less reckless than their counterparts all over the world. The only difference is that here they have a terrific advantage since there are so few cars on these enormously wide streets (Oh, wide avenues, where are you when we need you so desperately in New York?) They can work up a terrific speed and careen around corners scattering pedestrians, of which there are a great number.

The taxi is not new, not in tip-top shape mechanically, and although the spirit might be willing, certainly that of the driver, our car chokes and sputters to such a degree that we can only at last unclench our teeth and look out the window when we see us land in front of the Mockba Hotel.

Inside, chaos reigns. There are the usual Film Festival banners and posters, and manned desks hyping everything from the latest movie, to professional magazines and newspapers. We stagger from one "bureau" to another in the vast Entrance Hall, waving our official letter in front of anyone who will pay attention to us. We finally find someone who 1) speaks English and 2) can help us.

An hour later we have some kind of badge and packet of papers, and we're taken up in an enormous elevator to the seventh floor, (we try to find out to say "7" in Russian, so that we'll be able to get back on our own), then down a corridor, which, without exaggeration, is the length of a football field, and almost as wide, to a door which opens into a large entry hall, which gives into a room which could, in a pinch, if half the furniture were removed, serve as a very decent ballroom.

We are shown a huge (Help, I'm running out of adjectives for "big") bathroom with, for the very first time since we left home, our very own bathtub. The fact that it sits in a wooden frame, will easily accommodate guests, and is so deep I'm wondering where the ladder is to help me climb up to get in, does not in any way diminish its appeal, especially since we are again covered in several layers of grit and grime from the train ride. We had noticed the smart passengers sitting in their compartments with the windows shut tight ...

The two closets are room-size, but have no hangars. There is also the biggest *armoire a glace* I have ever seen. What irony, just when I only brought a suit, one dress, and one skirt. (no mink coat),

There is a slightly worn oriental rug on the floor, red satin damask floor-to-ceiling drapes, and orange chiffon ruffled bedspreads covering czar-size twin beds, with giant pillows stuffed to capacity. Next to the beds are bed tables, with rather ornate lamps and nearby, a dressing table and bench.

At one end of the room is what I suppose is meant to be the social-work area, with a two-seat sofa, two armchairs, a large round table covered with a white linen cloth, holding a crystal decanter with two crystal glasses on a silver tray, a sizeable desk, chair, and a T.V. set. One could also hold impromptu concerts because a good part of this "coin: as the French say, is taken up by a grand piano labeled "G Goetze St. Petersburg."

The paintings covering the walls are mostly landscapes, and have obviously not come from the Hermitage. Nor have the chandeliers, which I doubt were beautiful when new and have not improved with age. There is a radio playing Russian folk-melodies, but we can't seem to find the source. Russian Musak?

Floor to ceiling doors open onto a balcony, and we see a little box holding what looks like a tiny, sick bird. We wonder if it is being cared for by a chambermaid, and if we should share some of our penicillin with it, but decide not to interfere with its therapy and promise ourselves to watch its progress while we are here.

After initiating the bathtub, (I took the desk chair in, got up on my knees, and then managed to get up and into the tub. Bob, with his long legs was able to maneuver in by himself). We dress, and will try to find our way back downstairs to the Entrance Hall.

Leaving our room we notice two very no-nonsense women, one seated at each end of the hall. One of these stops us as we try to walk nonchalantly past her. She finds our names in the ledger on the table in front of her, makes some marks, and then has us understand that we are to check in and out with her every time we enter or leave our room. Rather than be shocked at this kind of control we choose to think of it from her point of view. She is too far from the woman at the other end for any kind of conversation, and if you were to sit in that big empty corridor all day long, you'd be sure to want a few words with anyone passing by.

Once downstairs it is again a quest to find someone who can tell us where to find the InTourist Office, since we feel obligated to check in with them and tell them I have arrived.

This turns out to be near the hotel. The woman there is very kind and helpful, and besides telling us not to be concerned about my "special arrangements", gives us a list of recommended restaurants, but suggests we stick to the hotel as much as possible. There is a message in there somewhere, but we choose to try to figure that one out later.

Back at the hotel we're in luck, as we're spotted by a French-speaking Russian official who wants to practice or show off his French. Either way we're ahead, because he takes us by the arms and leads us up and down several stairs and round-about, will we ever be able to find it again? to the restaurant, then disappears, telling us to wait until he returns with the head of the Festival Food Committee. Not only does he speak French, but has direct access to VIPs. When he returns we're suitably impressed, and try to thank him, sincerely appreciating his efforts on our behalf, but also to maintain the relationship for the obvious benefits it entails.

He dashes off, in such a way as to demonstrate that he has other important missions, and we're left with the Festival Food Committee Chairman, who sits down with us at a table and spends at least fifteen minutes explaining procedure involving coupons we were given, then taking our order personally. He insists we order only one meal, and that I share Bob's portion. I feel this is rather tacky and protest, but he assures us that this is protocol, and waves aside any and all objections. Shouldn't I even pay a cover charge? One more patronizing guffaw, and he is gone.

We're served an enormous meal, two plates, and what looks like portions not for two, but easily for four or more. Double desserts, endless cups of chai, and we roll out almost two hours later wondering who is starving in Russia, and if this is the way they feed tourists no wonder.

We take several wrong turns, and wish they had given us a good map of the hotel, but eventually find our way back downstairs and get right to work again trying to find out where the film showings take place. Three offices and five "interpreters" later we're shoved at the English speaking Head Interpreter of the Jury, Arthur, who takes us in his car to the Kremlin Theater. Each time we're led someplace we desperately try to memorize the route, not being able to count on the good fortune of an escort back.

We wave our passes, wander in, find seats

and-glory-be-earphones! However, our initial euphoria rapidly turns to frustration as we realize it is almost impossible to see, much less hear the film, juggling all the equipment, trying to lower the original sound track which is audible under the very hammy and amateur reading the translator is struggling to provide and is obviously having great difficulty in keeping up with.

Message: If one is seriously going to pursue film festivals with any sort of passion, Learn Lots Of Languages.

Including Czech. First film is Czechoslovakian, "Escape From The Shadows." Next, the French "Babette Goes To War".

We walk back to the hotel, across Red Square, get up to the 7th floor, check in with Our Lady Of The Ledger, pull back the orange chiffon bedspreads, hear the chimes strike one o'clock, and fall into bed telling each other yet again, "My Lord, we really are in Moscow"

Friday, August 7

Remember Cynthia, a working journalist, friend of a friend in Paris? She wakes us up early. We had left her a note telling her we had arrived. It turns out she is in a room just down the hall, tiny compared to our ballroom. We all wonder if we get the VIP treatment because we are representing a university–with students to influence- than she does writing for the capitalist New York Times?

We thank her profusely for insisting at the Cannes Festival that we try to get accredited to this Festival. And we apologize for not phoning her when we were back in Paris, explaining that all our time was taken up trying to recover the things that were stolen in front of the Place de L'Odeon.

Over breakfast – yes they serve caviar with our toast and tea – we get caught up on all her news. (Her husband, Richard, has stayed in Paris to work on his book.) Then we all go out together and we follow her around as she tries to find the telegraph office to send off her copy to the N.Y. Times.

Walking down the street near the hotel, we're approached by a young, good-looking, Russian boy who says, in perfect English, "I hear you're speaking English, are you Americans?"

This turns out to be the start of a remarkable friendship as we spend the next several hours listening to him pour his Russian heart out and ask us dozens of questions about "how it really is. We invite him to come back to the hotel and have lunch with us, and he does, because even though we see he feels very uncomfortable and keeps looking around suspiciously, he can't let us go.

We finally break up around four o'clock, promising to meet again, and then rush off to check in at the American Embassy. Cars are at our disposal in front of the hotel at all times, with drivers who sit around, sleeping on their arms, waiting their turn to be called. The problem is, trying to make ourselves understood.

The Embassy people tell us there are always Russian police guarding the entrance and they won't let any Russians enter the Embassy. The flag cannot be flown except on special holidays, and most personnel live on the premises.

We tell them about Dima, our new friend. They suggest that he simply doesn't know how dangerous it is to be seen with us, or else he is "one of them." Nevertheless, they very generously give us records and books to take to him. They seem a rather relaxed group, and tell us to come back if we need anything else.

Cleverly, we kept the taxi waiting because it's another rush back to the hotel – to change for the British Producers Reception at the Pravda Hotel. Lots of caviar, champagne, wine: Russian white, and Georgian red, strawberry ice cream with fresh strawberries, and coffee. Funny combination, but delicious. Two Russian newspapermen talk to us about the American Exhibition. They are disappointed because there aren't many new things, and hardly any tools and machinery. "We already know American cars are good, so why send cars?"

We also meet a couple from the British Embassy. He is much taken with one of the British starlets, and is hanging on her every giggle, while wife does not exhibit any of the famous British Reserve, as she openly sneers her disapproval.

Everyone is overjoyed at the success of their Tommy Sands, the Rock singer who seems to have knocked Moscow youth on its heels with his comments on TV this morning. He apparently ended his interview with something like, "And the best of British luck to you!" For some strange reason this really wowed them at the British Embassy.

At a given signal, of which we are completely unaware, everyone rushes out and into cars, and we're swept along with the crowd. I somehow end up with the Embassy Couple and Starlet, and it becomes more and more apparent during the ride that Mrs. Embassy Couple is not going to stand for much more of Mr. Embassy Couple's gaga infatuation.

However, as we all get out in front of The Friendship House, it is Miss Starlet herself who panics and makes a terrible scene, saying over and over again, stamping her foot with her voice, "I'M NOT GOING TO QUEUE! We're not going to have to queue, are we?" I WON'T QUEQUE – I'll go home first!" Clearly, Mr. E.C. would cut off his wrist before allowing her to do that, so leaving Mrs. E.C. and me in the lurch, he surges ahead, hustling Miss S. right through the crowds, and presumably into the safety of The Friendship House.

When Mrs. E.C. and I, I've lost Bob and Cynthia long ago, finally work our way inside, we find a very crowded room, a band playing very western "swing", and in another room more food and drink, with several officials trying to make toasts and give welcome speeches in front of a screeching mike. It's a very hot night, they are sweating, and almost no one is paying attention to them, having discovered and started to eat the food on the tables.

We eventually work our way close enough to see that there are the ubiquitous cookies, some pitifully small and brown-bruised apples, not too many grapes, candies, wines, fruit juices, and strange beige, vinegar-looking and tasting, cider perhaps, or a kind of fermented apple juice, in decanters on all the tables.

I spot Bob wandering around trying to find someone to talk to and see him establishing contact with a dark haired, sloe-eyed temptress wearing a sexy black dress and a patch over one of those sloe-eyes.

Meanwhile, Mrs. E.C. and I have found two of the few available seats in the middle room. We have mutual complaints: our errant husbands, which we don't discuss, and tired feet, which we do. Her husband makes a brief appearance and she sublimates her displeasure by giving him hell for putting his wine glass down on a marble topped table. "It will stain, you idiot!" He only came up to tell her "We must get Carol to her TV show by ten o'clock, let's leave <u>now</u>!" And they take off, to indulge in further family dramas. I wish them "The Best of British Luck," but I don't think they hear me.

An Indian Producer's children take her place on the settee next to me and we have a lively chat about how many brothers and sisters they have, their ages, etc. This carries us nicely along until their mother appears. I ask her if she knows our Indian-film-maker-friend-from-Hollywood. She knows all the producers in India, she announces, but his name isn't familiar. This puts a damper on the conversation; I certainly can't ask her how many brothers and sisters she has, much less her age. But at that point a Mr. Dobrochof joins us and I sparkle with my impressions of Moscow and the Festival, until I find out that he is the Head of the Festival, then am so preoccupied with trying to remember just what I said and if I made any blunders, that I no longer sparkle.

Cynthia, who has built in antennae for any and all news worthy names, certainly a notable asset in her profession, has spotted Dobrochof and makes a bee-line for him, and only because I'm standing next to him, me. And just as I'm wondering how I can possibly add to this new conversation, Bob appears at last, and whips me off to the dance floor in what turns out to be Exhibition Dancing. The spectators think it's rock 'n' roll, but I know it's really a 1948 version of the New Yorker. Photographers are snapping photos of us, everyone seems impressed, so why argue?

I never find out anything about Miss One-Sloe-Eye, other than "I think she's one of the Hungarian actresses' mother. They say she's a big character, but I couldn't get much out of her." Just what exactly did he want?

Cynthia has, in the meantime, picked up the French Entourage, and I must say they make quite a glamorous scene as we all leave. The actress, Nicole Courcel, in the lead, in a dashing backless gown, with her blond hair swept into a complicated swirl, whisks us along with them to try to find "The American Club in the heart of Moscow" which isn't much for directions, but somehow we manage to find it. It's a private club for Americans and Canadians who are stationed in Moscow. There's a bar, juke box, dancing, movies, TV, a library, nothing extraordinary, but the French are simply smitten with it all. Strange indeed that the French have found their closest look yet of the U.S. in the middle of Moscow.

Later, we walk for blocks trying to find taxis. My feet are screaming at me, and again I'm separated from Bob and Cynthia, and am with a very short French producer who asks me in French if I know the address, and I say yes, thinking he's asking if I'm going to ride in the cab which has just arrived. Moments of great confusion until Nicole turns and asks me in impeccable English if I have a map or know the address of another club everyone seems eager to investigate. I'm no help at all, even beginning to pout considering that Nicole could have lessened my language struggles many times tonight, and the fact that my feet are killing me.

After more discussion of which I understand very little, our taxis roar around Moscow and pull up in front of a building. We all get out, the taxis leave, and someone announces that whatever it is, is closed.

The streets now look even wider and emptier than ever. It's after one o'clock as we start walking, and I can't even ask if anyone knows if we're headed in the right direction because I doubt if anyone knows what the right direction should be. The only salvation for my feet now is amputation. Nicole takes off her black satin shoes and walks in stocking feet. I would follow suit and remove mine except that 1) I fear by now they're glued to my feet and 2) I don't have another pair of nylons.

What a group we make: a roly-poly fat producer, a handsome dark young man with a camera around his neck, a handsome blond young man without a camera, a cute brunette, blond Nicole, and we three Americans, Bob, Cynthia, and I.

The few people on the streets stare, then actually start to follow us as we see a sign, which clever Bob figures out, says "Metro" and we all head in that direction. They stand and watch as Nicole spots a lone woman behind small wagon, and stops to buy ice cream for everyone, not too easy when she is also holding her beautiful shoes. She ends up kissing the withered face of the old woman, "Isn't her face wonderful?!"

Someone throws Nicole a flower, and we walk into the Metro. It is HUGE! An escalator going as far down as one can see. It almost vanishes at the bottom. Lights along the walls are attractive and add to the feeling of length. I very nearly get an attack of vertigo just standing at the top and looking down.

We ride down, only to find that the train we think we want leaves from the top floor, so we ride back up, the two trips taking at least ten minutes. I sit down on the way up, why not if it's going to take so long? The photographer is taking lots of photos, the blond Frenchman sticks his finger in one of the dozens of jets in the spectacular water fountain, which we all think is hilarious, but the Russians still following us don't laugh as water sprays all over the floor.

The coaches are like train coaches, they're very clean and comfortable, but what is really shocking is not to see any ads – anywhere. Can't decide if this is good or bad. I think I actually miss them, but feel I shouldn't.

When we finally get back to the Mockba Hotel, most of our group wants to go up to the Midnight Bar, but Cynthia, Bob, and I beg off, Cynthia to write, Bob to bed, and I to pry off my shoes and try to recover in a hot bath.

It has been, shall we say, A Full Day. In Moscow.

Saturday, August 8

I feel brave enough to head off by myself to check out GUMS, Moscow's answer to Macys. Another huge four-story, block-large building, interior glass dome ceiling, fountain in center of first floor (adding more humidity to this hot weather), all very impressive.

There are the usual ice-cream and fruit juice vendors. The crowds are not polite, as they push, shove, and elbow; their muscular strength is considerable. Too often I find myself nailed to the floor by sturdy Russian shoes.

There isn't too much merchandise, but the only department that is entirely empty is the Toy Department, so I use this as a refuge, returning to it to catch my breath whenever I get another attack of claustrophobia in the aisles. Masses of Chinese are buying all the aluminum pots and pans on display. I give up on the third floor, and this should go on record as one of the few times in my life, if not the only one, in which I entered and left a major department store without making a purchase. Very disconcerting, and I reconsider going back in to buy, if nothing else, a chocolate bar, except I noticed all the candy was imported from Czechoslovakia.

Back to the hotel in time for the Polish reception. More caviar, ice cream, wine, cakes, fruit, etc. We meet a Finnish producer, very nice, who invites us to visit his studio in Helsinki on our return to Stockholm. Bob drags over a Mexican director and expects me to conduct a pertinent conversation with him in Spanish. I'm so preoccupied struggling to recall my high school Spanish, and all I can come up with are lists of fruits and vegetables, that I don't introduce Cynthia when she appears. Seconds later she launches into fluent Spanish, chitter-chattering away, while I'm still on naranjas (oranges), manzanas (apples), and platanos (bananas). Turns out she worked in Madrid for a couple of years. I withdraw, not gracefully.

Dima finds Bob and me in the hotel lobby and we have a few minutes to make plans for tomorrow before we go back to the Kremlin theater to see East German films. There we turn off our simultaneous translations and doze comfortably.

As we walk back across Red Square, we stop to watch the Changing of the Guard in front of the Lenin-Stalin tombs, crowded even at this late hour. There is a lot of heavy stomping around by the guards, but considering they have been standing for four hours, it seems a good way to stimulate their circulation

The few taxis, buses, and state cars (hardly any private autos, bikes, or scooters), have the entire vast square to rattle around in, while hundreds of shoving pedestrians push ahead on the sidewalks, giving each other and us nasty bruises. What they ought to do is let the pedestrians use the streets and move the automotive traffic, such as it is, onto the sidewalks.

There is yet another movie being projected outdoors on the other side of the square, but a hot bath in our swimming pool of a tub, and bed win out.

Sunday, August 9

We're told to be downstairs by 9 AM where buses are waiting to take us to The Boathouse. When we board the buses we find paper bags on each seat containing two pi-roshkies (baked meat pastries), a sandwich, and piece of fruit (what, no caviar?) Pretty hearty way to begin the day.

The Boathouse turns out to be yet another huge, stadium-like building, through which we are marched onto one boat, which we cross, then step over to another boat alongside. This one is very plush, blue damask wall covering, polished brass.

Cynthia is with the French entourage, so we wander on and have breakfast – guess the contents of those paper bags were just meant to keep us from fainting from hunger before we boarded - with the Austrian delegation. Bob is sitting next to someone who wants to teach him the secrets of the Russian alphabet and proper pronunciation. We all bemoan the fact it's so difficult to get any information in Russia. How is it possible there are no telephone books, maps, or guide books?

It's a nice, warm, sunny day, there are many people bathing in the canal, waving at us waving at them. A few boats pass us as we chug along. I keep waiting for something to happen, or for us to reach a special site, but around noon we get to a large opening in the canal, turn around and head back.

We talk to Mauno, our Finnish producer friend, then meet the author of a recently published book on the Battle of Stanlingrad, which was made into movie in East Berlin, and which we promise to see. There is folk dancing on the lower deck, where Giulietta Masina is holding court, and I take out my camera hoping to capture a good photo. She is one of my favorite actresses and I'd like to tell her so, but don't think I could get through the energetic folk dancers surrounding her. She doesn't seem to be in a great mood, maybe because she'd like to get through them also.

Later we go in for lunch and spot a table with one man and a couple of empty seats. He answers my questioning glance with a nod, we're getting used to language barriers. Bob and I have a quiet chat about evening plans, mentioning the possibility of going to the N.Y Times correspondent, Max Frankel's apartment for cocktails.

In one long pause I turn to ask the man at our table if he speaks English. He answers that English is about all he speaks, and that he has been sitting there listening to us and wondering how long he was going to be able to hold out before speaking.

We tell him what we're doing in Europe, and he tells us he is Preston Grover, of Associated Press. They are doing a story on the American Exhibition, would we like to write a short five hundred-word article on The Tourist's Impression of the American Exhibition? For pay, of course.

I gulp and Bob answers, "Yes, of course, we'd love to." He says he'll drop off passes for us, adding, "Don't make it sound too professional, you're supposed to be ordinary tourists. I want to assure him that he definitely needn't worry about that, but I don't.

By the time we work our way through the Mexican contingent, producers, photographers, and a couple of actors, this time I can at least manage a "Buenas Dias", then wonder if it isn't "Tardes" by now, we dock, climb in and over boats and get back on shore.

A quick stop at the hotel to tidy up, change into proper cocktail attire, which for me is a too warm for this weather, but proper looking suit, and go with Cynthia to Max Frankel's apartment. Mrs. Frankel gives us a rather cool reception, takes Cynthia aside, whispers in her ear, Cynthia comes back to tell us she misunderstood the invitation, it seems to be for diner and there isn't enough for us, and we should more or less leave gracefully.

So we chat quickly with the other nice newspaper people in this New York-in-Moscow apartment, complete with Danish teak furniture imported from Copenhagen, and take our leave, more disgruntled then gracious.

Back to the hotel we go straight to the dining room and order dinner. Just starting on the caviar – I thought I would never tire of caviar, but I'm beginning to reconsider – when Dima comes in, all dressed up in white shirt, tie, etc. We see that he is disturbed and ask him to sit down. Then he tells us 1) he and his friend, Tolya, have been waiting for us on our floor lobby for an hour, having had to do battle with Our Lady Of The Ledger, who asked them why they were there, and not satisfied told them to leave, and 2) his wife has made dinner for us.

Our explanation: yes, we had made plans yesterday, but he didn't pursue them and we didn't want to pressure him, so when he didn't phone at five o'clock as we had arranged, we assumed he had decided against our going to his house.

We tell him to please explain to the waiter that we can't finish our meal, leave with him immediately, and go to meet smiling Tolya. A walk together across Red Square to catch a bus, and as we ride, then walk again, Dima explains that we are going to his and Natalia's flat which really belongs to her parents, but they are away in the country. Her father is a retired army officer, which is how they have such a large and comfortable apartment. When we arrive, enter, and stumble over the bed in one of two rooms, we can only wonder how the less well-placed people live.

The other room has a wall to wall bed; the kitchen and bathroom are tiny, but Dima reiterates how fortunate they are, telling us how, while waiting for many years to get their own apartment, he and his parents lived in one room, sharing one kitchen and one bathroom with ten other families.

He complained, "People are the same everywhere, and when something doesn't belong to you there is no pride or interest in keeping it clean, so it was always dirty, terribly dirty. My mother kept after the other women to clean up the kitchen, but it just wasn't any good and we talked night after night how we could get a place of our own." His descriptions of the miseries of ten families sharing one bathroom were equally dismal.

His father is a party line chemist and earns three thousand rubles a month, which is a substantial income. There just aren't enough apartments or houses, available, nor for that matter, meat, decent produce, clothing, in short consumer goods and comforts.

Natalia is blond, sweet, smiling, and has very pretty eyes. She motions us to help ourselves to the food on the table. Dima wants us to understand they have prepared a normal, typical dinner so we can see how they really live, and if they were ever to visit us in the United States, he would expect us to do the same for them.

There is a large pot of boiled potatoes with what looks like a full pound chunk of good butter, along with lots of fresh bread. This is what they eat with great gusto. There are also dishes of sliced cabbage and carrots, a few tomatoes, a can of sardines, and squares of a cold meat stock gelatin, but since they don't touch any of this I can assume they are there for our benefit, in spite of what he says.

Dima disappears into the kitchen and returns, proudly bearing a dish of melting ice cubes. He heard us say how much we enjoyed the ice-water dispenser at the American Embassy, and he thought he would try to "make some ice-water for us," but he didn't know how, would we teach him? Once we have the ice cubes in the glasses with water, he sips it as if he were tasting some precious French vintage wine. Approving, he nods to Natalia ordering her to provide this for all their meals in the future. We try to point out that they might not want to carry on this "American Custom" in the dead of their winter, nor should it necessarily replace tea or coffee in the morning. After all, one feels responsible exporting certain rituals and customs.

Dima is translating for Tolya and Natalia, but gets caught up in trying to explain to us that it isn't the lack of proper housing, difficult as it is, nor the need for better food and clothing – this he feels people can do without, if they have to. It is all the other things they don't have which is so hard to bear. There isn't a western publication to be had, other than the Communist papers of France, East Germany, etc.

Aside: the head of the Festival Jury, one of a seven man team writing a new definitive English-Russian dictionary, pleaded with us yesterday to get him a copy of TIME – "Not for the subject matter, you understand, but to pick up some slang..."

Dima continued: the people can travel within Russia, if they have good reasons and don't stay too long. They must register when they arrive, take care of their business and return home again with no delays. They can't, of course, leave the country. When we tell Dima about the countries we have visited and going to see he says, "To me, such a thing is like a dream – unbelievable." We tell him it's like a dream to us too, but for different reasons.

They turn on Voice of America in English – the Russian version is jammed, and Dima translates for Natalia and Tolya. Next they play their two rock 'n' roll records and ask us to dance for them. Again, it isn't really rock 'n' roll, but they like it and we try to teach them our version.

When we leave, Dima walks with us and Tolya to find a taxi. We want to drop Tolya at his home first, but he refuses and tells the driver to take us to our hotel – he's afraid we'll get lost otherwise.

Question: What can we do for these dear (good) people?

Monday, August 10

Breakfast is by now pretty routine: tomato juice: big glasses of kafir; a thin, buttermilk kind of yoghurt, served with sugar; two 3-minute eggs-at last the waiter and I agree on what this means. Others have jelly omelettes; huge sweet rolls, toast, butter, and if we can manage to get our coffee or tea at the same time, we can have strawberry jam, because the jam is meant to be dumped into the tea and coffee, and is never served with anything else.

The "American Table" is getting larger everyday as the word goes around that The Mockba Hotel is where all the good food is these days. "Try to get chocolate ice cream anywhere else in town..." The group so far includes screenwriter Paul Jericho, on the Hollywood blacklist, and his wife Sylvia, living and working in London; Alexander Parkson, correspondent for a string of Jewish papers; Bob Korengold, U.P. representative; Hans Von Nolde, A.P. photographer, originally sent to cover the Nixon tour, staying on for a short time to help out with the Exhibition; Gene Moskovitz, Variety correspondent from Paris; actress Dawn Addams with her official translator; "Napoli", an Italian American distributor who is upset because he wasn't asked to be Guilietta Massina's translator, and a couple of hanger-on translators, who all seem to be myopic and wear perfectly round, thin metal-framed glasses that are much too small and stretch out to barely hook around their ears.

A group of us walks over to St. Basils to push in through

the crowds of local tourists. There is an old man with a long, grey beard wearing a soiled tunic with knee-high boots looking just like a peasant in a Tolstoy novel, and we nod together as we strain to marvel at the onion domes, and the round chapels inside. Bob goes on to take photos of the Kremlin and have a crack at Gums. I'm starting to write post-cards: "Greetings from Moscow!"

Tuesday, August 11

Cynthia appears early to report that her talk out loud to herself in her room last night, assuming and hoping she had an unseen audience, was very effective. She complained about both lofty and practical things such as her bathroom plumbing which didn't work and which she had reported daily since arrival. A repairman was there first thing this morning.

Bob and Cynthia leave early for the Auto Factory Tour. Dima and I have a date to do the Kremlin, which is the most wonderful combination of glitter and grime. Like everything else it is huge. The scale of this country and everything in it is not easy to absorb, and spending a few hours "in the Kremlin" where hundreds of yards can separate one building from another, does not give me any right or ability to say more.

We regroup for lunch then spend most of the afternoon strolling through the streets, Dima stops talking only when he waits, sometimes impatiently, for the answers to his questions which we try to think through carefully and respond to with some substance and honesty, not always easy to do.

We stop in a famous bakery, famous because it used to make "the King's bread," and buy what looks like mandel bread but feels like stone, and a ginger cake and cookies, which are much better. We drink kasse, a vegetable root drink dispensed by an old woman sitting on a chair on the street, from a large tank on wheels. A hose, connected to a truck nearby, provides a shot of water to "clean" the three glasses in constant use.

Dima leads us to a window in an old wooden building to buy piping hot, king-size bagels, so hot we can hardly hold them, but so delicious we go back for more. Finally coffee at a sidewalk cafe. Dima tells us the waiters want and need tips, contrary to InTourist information and advice. We walk back to the hotel in a cold wind-an indication that winter comes early here?

After dinner Bob and I stand around the lobby next to Richard Todd, who is trying to find transportation to the theater. We join him in the car pool line. Bob obviously doesn't recognize him as he asks, "What do you do?" I try to cover, countering with "What day will your film be shown?" which erases his frown only slightly. One shouldn't mess with actors' egos. I charge on, introducing us, "…from Film Quarterly", hoping that will move us up his scale enough to answer my next chatty question, "Have you been to the Gypsy Restaurant everyone is talking about?" and he actually smiles as he says he has and it was "Goodish". Stay Still, My Thumping Heart, he really is very handsome.

And now very charming as he tells us just as he learned how to say "6" in Russian he was moved to the 5th floor. But rather than try to learn a new number he still goes to the 6th and walks down. I say it's "'*Pieta*' and by that time you need it", but no one seems to hear the pun, as a girl rushes up to tell him his car is ready. He turns to us and offers to let us take it. "Are you quite sure?" "Yes, yes", he replies, "We're waiting for others and by the time they get here the car will be back". We thank him and go off in the rain with a couple of Bulgarians who somehow get in on the deal.

As it turned out, the film we were hoping to see had been screened that afternoon. So we sit through a Mongolian film-I think it's a western. I try to concentrate but all I want to do is return to the room for chai. Which, eventually, I do. But all that arrives is pots of hot water, and I'm forced to use my remaining tea bag. Only when that is brewed, ready to drink, does a lady wearing a floppy white cap knock at the door with four! And more pots. This time brimming with chai.

Wednesday, August 12

After breakfast Bob visits a Russian Animation Studio and Cynthia and I go to the Vassily Theater, yet another venue not too easily reached, to see some old Russian short films. Again, no information available, no translations, and not much interest, so we leave quickly and find our way to the American Embassy. Mission: pick up as many books and records as we can carry, as well as very scarce tickets to the American Exhibition, for Dima and Tolya, all of which we deliver when we go back to Dima's apartment.

But if we thought we were loaded arriving, we can hardly make it leaving with all the gifts they give us: dozens of records of Russian folksongs, Russian dolls, small and large porcelain figurines, and a small porcelain rabbit which Natasha tells me she is especially fond of. Tolya, not wanting to be outdone, hands us an enormous plastic model airplane he made.

Dima hands us a large envelope of his paintings. He confesses he heard about "abstract painting", but didn't know what it was, and couldn't find any reproductions anywhere. But he read what he could and talked to a few painters, and with the limited supplies he has, secretly painted dozens and dozens of colorful, vivid rectangles, on cardboard. He has it all figured out: he will sign them with a false name, Dick Joy, just in case we're caught with them; we will take them out to show as many people as we can that there are people in the Soviet Union brave enough to paint politically unacceptable, even dangerous, art.

We have already discussed the possibility of further communication, at least our being able to write to him. We will send our letters either to someone in the Embassy, or one of the U.S. correspondents, who will readdress the envelopes in Russian, and mail them locally. We will eventually tell him how people liked his paintings. Our code? We will say that *Bob's* paintings were very successful.

He is so serious and determined we are shaken, and are host to feelings of anger, gratitude, responsibility, and love.

Thursday, August 13

After a quick caviar breakfast and foregoing conversation with the American Contingent, we rush to Sokolny Park and the American Exhibition early. Duty first: we take photos for Herman Miller. Cynthia grabs us and introduces us to Paddy Chayefsky, one of our heroes. We trade impressions: how wonderful that the U.S. seems to have done Something Right for a change. There are crews of poised, intelligent, bright-eyed, good-kid guides, who speak Russian, one and all. The signs are in Russian. The exhibitions are well presented, with plenty of space to accommodate the normal crowds.

Again, thanks to Cynthia, I find myself having a Demonstration Facial in the open-air beauty salon, while hundreds of very curious Soviet citizens, men and women, stand by watching all the slathering going on, and if there weren't a railing holding them back I fear they might surge forward to put their fingers in all the pots.

I always look lousy after one of these make-up jobs, sort of like I should put on tights and go out for the second act of Swan Lake, but when it's all finished my present audience applauds wildly at the results. Oh, well.

We meet Dima, Natalia, and Tolya on schedule and wheel them through the crowds to the most important exhibits. Dima has a headache so I lead him to a water fountain and give him a special kind of aspirin I carry, all of which attracts an enormous crowd that attentively watches each act of this seemingly interesting drama. Only when I have closed up my purse and we walk away does the crowd disperse.

It is almost impossible to go through the model home, and Nixon was clever in staging his "Kitchen Debates" here on very solid home ground, so to speak.

It's late afternoon before we leave, and we later plead with our normally cheery, but very slow waiter, to bring us our dinner quickly, Spaseva, Spaseva, so that we can get to the Puppet Theater in time for the evening performance.

We do, somehow, and I'm glad we didn't miss one single moment. No wonder they're so famous. I sit marveling at how they can capture so many nuances of character. No banging heads of snooping policemen here. My definition of puppets has been altered for all time, and my hands are sore from constant applauding.

Another Very Full Day.

Friday, August 14

Morning spent writing article for A.P. When we deliver it a photographer takes our photo to accompany the article. We all go over to Red Square, he hands us a fake Map of

Moscow-we all know they don't exist-has us look down at it, with our backs to St. Basil. After only a few shots, the usual crowd gathers to stand and watch the funny foreigners.

I go off to Lenin's Tomb, where I create a tremendous scene when I inadvertently "gate crash". Armed guards rush forward, then call for reinforcements! Sensing a serious lack of communication, I very politely try to make it very clear that <u>if</u> I can't get in now, (I hesitate to wave my passport around as we were told to do,) when <u>can</u> I see it?

By then, of course, the crowds have gathered. Who sends out signals? As I babble on, and point repeatedly to my watch, the people try to help me and start shouting at the guards who are by then just as confused as I am, but thankfully not trigger-happy. Finally one man surges forward and yells "Morgan"; I'm pretty sure that's the German for "tomorrow", or is it "morning"? Either way, I obviously can't get in today. I smile graciously, I trust, at one and all, and begin the long, hard push through the crowds, heading back to the relatively safe haven of the hotel.

Once again, Cynthia rounds up a crowd and we go to yet another reception. I find myself at one point trying to balance glasses of Georgian red wine, Russian white wine, local champagne, two coupettes of strawberry ice-cream with fresh strawberries on top, a plate of caviar, and two cups of coffee.

Let nothing be said of Russian hospitality, except maybe the generous combinations thereof.

We go to a Mexican Socialist-Comedy, strange genre, but we've given up on that score (Bulgarian Happy Farmer Meets Happy Tractor, result: Happy Tomatoes). The best part was gaping at the Mexican actress, Rosita Quintana, in her very striking Aztec finery

We can't find a taxi home, so we take a bus. We're

trampled, knocked down, shoved, and I almost break my glasses trying to get off. "The Russian Push." Will we live through it?

Saturday, August 15

At some point, when we considered ourselves prominent members of the film festival racket, we wrote and received invitations to the Venice Film Festival which starts next week. When we mentioned this to Cynthia she jumped for joy, suggested we join her on the train with stops in Warsaw and Vienna. We pointed out that when we replied to Venice we still had cash reserves, and a car available, neither of which we now have. Money, in fact, is getting lower to low. She countered that the car would not be of any use in Venice, and she knows all kinds of cheap places to stay, and that the usual festival spreads of cocktail food, spaghetti and fruit would see us through very well.

We'll see.

Bob goes to pick up tickets for tonight's Festival train trip to Leningrad. Dima helps me get into Lenin's Tomb at last. Very cold. Great embalming job.

Two old women wearing babushkas and men's jackets are standing outside holding out two pairs of fancy socks, which look Finnish. One motions to the other and they both quickly stuff the socks inside their jackets as two policemen walk by. Then they take out the socks again and continue their very private enterprise.

Back to the hotel for snacks, baths, pack, and check out in that order. Bob asks for the bill, and with some confusion the girl pulls out one of many envelopes held together with rubber bands, flips a few wooden counters on her abacus and charges him a total of 50 rubles. ($5.00) For everything? That's all? For both of us? She apologizes for the charge, isn't quite sure what it's for-scrambles around in dozens more envelopes like ours, smiles and says "O.K." several times, more to convince us than herself.

Maybe we will go to Venice with Cynthia after all.

We round up Cynthia and Variety correspondent, Gene Moskovitz, with whom we are sharing a compartment, and get to the station in time for the 12:30 night train to Leningrad. We order chai and raisin buns, sit in bed and sip hot tea as the radio plays Prokofiev and the train pulls out of the Moscow station. Grand!

Sunday, August 16

Sandwiches and hard mandel bread on the compartment table when we awaken at 7:30. Dress hurriedly for arrival in Leningrad at 8:00 AM. Lots of flowers and speeches on the platform. Once again Guilleta Massina looks tired and angry as she gives her "greeting", and we don't see her again.

Bus to hotel, where a large suite is waiting for the Americanski Delegazi. Bob conks out on one of the lace spread covered beds, I play the grand piano, and Gene dumps the flowers in the paws of an upright bear bronze statue on the desk.

Cynthia, Gene, and I go down to look for café-cafeteria, but everything looks especially unkempt, so we give up and wander through the Sunday streets. Quiet, much more dignified than Moscow. Many trees, canals, and lakes. Very weak shades, but shades nevertheless, of Paris.

Walk all the way to the Winter Palace and back, passing a closed, locked church, with shawl-covered older women kneeling in front of each door, then placing flowers in the grill work.

Breakfast waiting when we get back to the hotel. Then

into buses for the official tour. First the Hermitage, we're allotted two hours of wandering wherein Cynthia, Bob and I successfully lose our group and marvel in the endless masterworks before we realize we're quite lost in this gigantic building and rush around madly until we find the group again and sheepishly join them as they are filing out the door past TV cameras and crew who choose Bob and me to interview. They follow our buses in open cars as we pass monuments, famous ships, (Battleship Potemkin), Sunday bathers in old-fashioned underwear along the canals, sunning themselves. The ladies could use a Slenderella treatment and an updated Sears Catalog. The men need hair cuts. But they look brown, and healthier than we.

We're all drooping as we are dragged to the new Hero Stadium. Finally back to the hotel and our suite for showers. Dinner amongst the potted palms in the dining room, where food is the very same as the Mockba. Did they bring the chef along?

We dawdle and by the time we get outside all the buses have left. Momentary panic gives way to hearty congratulations as after a short scurry we're stashed into a carpeted limousine, stretch our bus-cramped legs, let the wind blow our hair through the open windows and watch the people on the country roads watching us fly by.

We rendezvous with the rest of the group at a Garden of Fountains-some former king's idea of jolly good fun, with over a hundred jokey fountains shooting out of the ground in unexpected places, out of fake fruit trees, over innocent looking benches, in a bizarre merry-go-round. Everyone on the verge of hysteria, more from exhaustion, I suspect, than awe.

It gets cool around 7 o'clock as we watch the sun go down in a haze over the Baltic Sea. Herded back on the bus-what happened to our limo? for the trip to some building in town where the local Film Society shows a film, (something about Leningrad Then and Now). Dull and hours long. Another reception. By now it's hot again, crowded as usual, lots of wine and brandy and sweets, as usual. I try to avoid the mayonnaise slathered offerings.

We're then taken back to the hotel for yet another meal. It's hard to know what to call it anymore, late dinner maybe? Pre-midnight snack? Finally bus to station, where we all fall in exhausted as the train pulls out at midnight.

Monday, August 17

Arrive Moscow 8:30, breakfast at the hotel. Decision has been made, we'll use our AP rubles, approximately $50, which, paying in rubles, should cover the cost of our train tickets Moscow-Warsaw-Vienna-Milan-Venice; Venice-Stockholm. Another What If – we hadn't had to sit at the same table as the AP representative??? (We can probably even get a refund on our return tickets Moscow-Helsinki-Stockholm.)

Bob and Cynthia go off to arrange tickets. My mission is to get our visas at the Czech and Polish embassies. I waste the first precious hour forgetting passport photos and having to return to hotel to retrieve them, thereby losing Nina, our translator, who was willing to help me if we were back by 11.

The Waiting Room in the Czech Embassy (old building, creaky wooden floors, high ceilings, French door-windows testifying to its former, long gone elegance, is a seething cauldron of frustration: dozens of people, some seething quietly, others not so; an American couple making a scene-"We have reservations for a hotel in Prague!"; the embassy official, harassed and hypertense, trying to tell their interpreter (although she speaks English to me), that this is impossible, she can give them a transit visa only and they must stay at the the airport hotel; the man insisting he has a hotel reserved in Prague; the woman screaming back that she has nothing to do with hotels, the interpreter standing in no-mans' land in the middle with a helpless smile on her face. I identify with her.

Meanwhile, my festival driver is waiting impatiently, my "five minutes" were up twenty ago. He comes in distraught. I try to tell him it shouldn't be too much longer. I dare not let him go because I've got to go to the Polish Embassy and haven't a clue where it is or how to get there.

I'm finally ushered into an inner sanctum, where a frazzled man listens to my pleas, with half-shut eyes, waiting not so patiently to deliver his memorized response which is almost a plea on his part: this is a very busy "season", they can only issue transit visas, and if I will leave our passports they will try to process them for us within 10 days.

TEN DAYS! I quite unintentionally break into tears. (the heat? the hurry? the crowds? the frustration? the time of the month? Who knows?)

Babbling, our train leaves at midnight, I still have to get our Polish visas. my husband is expecting me to do all this. What am I to do?

He suddenly comes to life, old gallantry genes surfacing wildly. He rushes to shut and bolt the door, glances around furtively, and then before my very eyes, papers are shuffled, drawers are opened and shut, fountain pen entries made as ledgers are opened and closed and, as I continue to sniffle, recognizing all too quickly my advantage in this particular chess game, stamps, glorious stamps, are pounded, pasted, and affixed to numerous papers and-glory be-our passports!

All that done, he files, opens and closes more drawers, shoving back all his accoutrements, then finally swoops up our passports, says, "They'll be ready this afternoon, come back at five."

Before he opens the door he leans over and as one conspirator to another says, "When you go to the Polish Embassy, be sure to tell them that the Czech Embassy processed your papers in less than an hour...that will make them try to do it faster!"

As I rushed out I heard him announce to the group at large, "IMPOSSIBLE, TOTALLY IMPOSSIBLE!"

The grumbling driver deposits me at the Polish Embassy and rushes off. Same kind of old building, up the stairs, in the back, another crowded room, some of the same faces I saw in the Czech Embassy. Same scene: Absolutely no visas issued today. Same panic, as I quietly, in soft, humble voice tell the same sort of frantic man the same story, we're leaving on the midnight train, and as the tears start to gush I add that I would have come earlier but I was at the Czech Embassy, and although they too were very busy they did process our applications in an hour and they'll be ready by five...

I am immediately ushered into an inner office, where the drawers begin to open and close again and, as I keep the tears moist and rolling, he mutters and mumbles, "Less than an hour? This is positively the very last today...fill out these forms...(stamp, stamp, stamp, stamp, stamp)..."Do not say *anything to anybody*!....and come back at *"four*, do you understand?, *not five, four o'clock!"*

I finally bring out my hanky and in all sincerity tell him "I hope an American will do something just as kind for you someday".

Two German students standing in front of the building

tell me what bus to take to get back to the hotel. I stop to take last few color photos, then march into the dining room triumphant over my Victory of the Visas. Cynthia is especially proud of me and my tactics. Bob is unimpressed, assuming all along I was capable of this to him minor mission. Next time _he_ goes.

Afternoon: last call to the American Embassy for books; Intourist to pick up train tickets, for some reason they cost less than Cynthia's; finally the Polish at four, and the Czech-at-five (fifteen minutes before they close) embassies, with long waits again, but enormous satisfaction as I leave with the coveted transit visas in hand.

We have a forty-eight-hour transit visa for Poland, and a no-stop transit visa for Czechoslovakia. So be it.

Back at the hotel, we pack up hurriedly, trade rest of meal coupons (meant for one, the two of us ate-to-bursting, and we still have many left over- (faulty calculations, or Russian generous hospitality?) for fruit. But the waiter thinks he is doing us a big favor by giving us mostly chocolate, the most expensive and unnecessary thing we want in Russia, or as provisions for a long train trip. But he is very, very sweet and has done wonders trying to understand our English and meal needs all this time. Bob gives him dollar bills which he asks Bob to sign. We hope he senses how much we like him and appreciated his gold filled smiles (everyone has gold or metal capped teeth).

Dima and Tolya arrive and we all sit in Gene's tiny room trying to joke, not wanting to leave and yet hoping the time will go by quickly to end this awkward Airport-Train-Station Syndrome). Finally, we load up our bags-it always seems as if we're traveling light until we have to carry our bags anywhere.

To the station. Cynthia finds her compartment. We're

with a Russian couple. Last minute "How do you say's?" from Tolya, take some movies, then a very tearful goodbye. How we wish we could see them again-somewhere-sometime. This is strangely final.

While we're feeling so low there is a fast shuffle taking place about which we're not even aware. The Russian couple has been moved out and a German, handsome and young, is throwing down his one small suitcase and string bag holding bread and two cans of beer. He says they don't want Russians to mix with foreigners. We see the Russian couple standing in the aisle and we shrug and smile to them, hoping they realize we had nothing to do with their move and that we're sorry about it. The man is wearing those ubiquitous striped pajamas that look like prison sleeping gear. It all makes me feel as if we've taken his bed away for the night, which we may very well have done.

The German is Erik, professor of Ancient History and Languages, on his way back from Afghanistan where he has been following the path of Alexander the Great. When Peter, the guy who was on the train with us coming in also appears, it begins to feel like a late 1930's Hitchcock movie, especially when we find Peter noticeably changed. On the way in he was very quiet, unwilling to comment except to laugh at our "spy theories." We said the hay stack at the border looked suspicious, he said it looked like hundreds of others we passed. Bob said the conductor told him to get off the seat, which he interpreted as he was not supposed to look out that window. Pete said conductor probably meant he wasn't supposed to stand on the seat, etc.

Now he is moved and shocked by people he has talked to and things he has seen. He is carrying a book on Marx with inconsistencies underlined, which he says Russians won't accept. They are full of misinformation and have no wish to see anything else. He asks us specific questions about treaties, etc. He has certain "facts" he wants to check out. Bob knows some of the dates-from his stamp collection, I suppose, but I'm no help.

Erick just listens, then resumes his role as compartment boss, arranging to trade another man who just appears, with Cynthia, who it seems has been installed in a compartment filled with crying children. He shuffles the man out, ignorant of the fate awaiting him in the move, and with the help of Peter and Bob, brings Cynthia and her "light" luggage, including typewriter, back to our compartment. She is near tears with relief.

The good part of all this moving around the train is that they discovered a diner, and we all go for a light supper-something with far too much mayonnaise for such a hot night. Back to the compartment for more talk. Previously quiet Peter can't stop. Finally to sleep.

Tuesday, August 18

Breakfast in the diner. Dirty tablecloth, flies in and on everything. Half-liter of kefir helps somewhat, so does the chai (although there's a fly in it too.) Cynthia orders blinis. They're meat-filled, and very greasy. We live through it nevertheless.

Read and talk until we arrive in Brest around 1 o'clock. Erick knows his way around and guides us quickly to make reservations for the next train, get in the customs line, etc. Then as the train pulls in he rushes off to save a compartment for all of us.

But they won't give our passports back to us. The train leaves and we never see Erik again-or our reserved seats. Pity, he was so helpful, maybe in some remote former life he really was an Alexander the Great groupie. We stand and sit helplessly, no one seems to know what is going on. If there were anyone to ask we would. Very strange. Is it because I have Tolya's model airplane under my arm? Vital aircraft secrets smuggler?

Finally Bob finds a girl who listens to our story and pleas, rushes away, then returns to tell us we're "delayed" because we entered the Soviet Union in Viborg-why are we leaving through Brest? Cynthia flew in-why is she taking the train out? Very serious questions and they have to phone Moscow for instructions.

We miss another train at 4 o'clock.

At what at some time or another had been, or would, one day, be a Station Buffet, we buy ice-cream, cookies, and cellophane bags containing yellowish hard-boiled eggs, tomatoes, bread, and some kind of terrible looking sausage.

I take a few photos, we're already in trouble so a few photos couldn't make things much worse, and try not to give in to grim scenarios of Incarceration in Brest. These become increasingly difficult to resist after they motion us into a customs room with all our baggage and tell us we are not to leave the room.

But Fearless Bob will not wait longer than ten or fifteen minutes, mumbles something like "this is ridiculous", and goes to check "on the situation". The 3:30 train, which we have been told is the last train to Warsaw today, pulls into the station. Simultaneously our girl, whom we are beginning to think of as our own personal savior, (she is, after all, the only one who not only talked to us, but actually found out answers to our questions, and even better, seemingly tried to do something about "the situation".) waves our passports, tells us they finally got through to Moscow, and because we were officially invited guests, we have permission to leave, but it is Very Irregular, and we must never do this again (!) And begins shoving our luggage through customs. We hold our breath-we're taking out rubles (Bob and his coin collection), Dima's paintings, and, of course, Toyla's unconcealed Soviet war plane model. No problem. She hands us our passports - we watch the train lurch forward then stop momentarily. We throw ourselves and luggage on the train and collapse in a very comfy upholstered compartment.

We barely have time for a sigh or two of relief when the conductor comes to tell us this is a first-class compartment and we're obviously second. So it's into a noisy, crowded car. Cynthia and I squeeze into seats with a French communist crowd, drinking wine and burping loudly. Cynthia says it's a blessing I can't understand them and their drivel. Loud, horsey laughing. Bob stands in the back with the luggage, sulking, uncomfortable, and covered with grime.

The train turns out to be a milk-run, and stops at every village. I take the "hand-luggage": records, books, camera, purse, magazines, etc. and put them on my lap, then try to read Cynthia's book on Poland while she tries to sleep. The train finally slows down, moves back and forth, and then backs into the Warsaw station, about 9 PM, and getting dark fast.

A DAY AT THE FAIR
by Bob and Cima Balser

We visited the American Exhibition here in Moscow today.
We were pushed, shoved, elbowed, stepped on by some sturdy
Russian boots, and we loved it !
Fortunately, the exhibition is laid out in a spacious park
and can accommodate the masses of people that are swarming
through, looking at what we have to show them.
At two o'clock in the afternoon there were incredibly long,
twisting lines of people waiting to see the Brotherhood of
Man exhibit, Circarama, and the Eames Seven-Screen Projec-
tion.
As we walked around we were impressed with how well done
the exhibition is by any standards - and here in Moscow,
especially, where everyone is unbelievably curious about
the United States, it's a smash hit.
We saw people scrambling to get any brochures, pamphlets,
and "reclams", they could get their hands on - including
copies of a booklet about Abraham Lincoln, in Russian.
Women were reading the Sears and Roebuck catalogues with
searing intensity.
And one of the most gratifying things to us, by far, was
to see hundreds of people pouring over the books which are
on open shelves for all to see, pick-up, and read if possible.
Many of the books are by now battered almost beyond repair

-2-

and we noted with personal satisfaction that *Freud, Vol. I* was missing.

Since we had heard that the major criticism of the exhibition coming from the Russian press here had been the lack of tools and machinery and the too large display of cars (which they say they already know are good), it was interesting to see that hardly anyone more than paused to look at the tractors, while we saw men duck under the ropes to have their pictures taken, smiling, standing next to a Ford !

One of us sat in curled wonder under a dryer in the open-air beauty salon, while literally hundreds of people, both men and women waited patiently to see the results. Some took notes.

As the day wore on, one word kept popping up again and again - "sensible". Sensible to have the pots and pans, groceries, clothing - all the paraphenalia of America out in the open, unguarded, for all to see, and more important, to touch. Such things are being carefully handled, inspected, and put back in place.

Sensible to have a plump, white-haired mother in the fashion show, and how she is wowing the babushka crowd !

Sensible to have a crew of freshly scrubbed, bright guides to answer Russian questions - and while we could only guess at what was being said, we could see the intensity with which our guides were being physically and verbally pushed against the wall, or a surrealistic painting, as the case may be, and at all times they seemed poised, fairly relaxed,

-3-

and well in control of the situation.

They, and the exhibition, are answering all the questions people have been stopping us personally in the streets to ask - "Are people starving in the United States? Are they laid-off work and thrown out of their homes? Does everyone live in slums? What does New York look like?"

We couldn't have asked for a more beautiful and honest answer to all their questions.

Everyone in Moscow these days is wearing a USA button from the exhibition. So are we.

AP Article of the American Exhibition

Moscow Film Festival
Cultural Ministry
Moscow, U.S.S.R.

Gentlemen:

We are presently in Europe representing FILM QUARTERLY
magazine, published by the University of California Press,
Berkeley, California, U.S.A.

We have just covered the 12th International Film Festival
at Cannes, France, and were happy to hear at that time
that the Moscow Film Festival had been accorded full
international recognition.

We are very interested in attending the Moscow Film
Festival and would appreciate information on what
arrangements can be made.

Since we are constantly traveling, please send whatever
information that is now available to the following
address:

        Mr. and Mrs. Robert E. Balser
        c/o American Express
        11 Rue Scribe
        Paris, France

Thank you very much for your attention to this matter.

Yours truly,

Robert E. Balser

REB/cb

May 25, 1959

Letter to the Moscow Film Festival

Postcard of Moskba Hotel

Train Tickets August 17th, 1959

Moscow, Warsaw, Czechoslovakia, Vienna,
Venice, and return to Stockholm

19

48 Hour Transit Visa to Poland Warsawa Diary

August 18ᵗʰ

As we leave the train Cynthia gives us instructions: I'll stand and watch the baggage, as she and Bob go into the station to find out about a hotel, change money, etc.

They return quarter of an hour later to report there's no place to change money and no hotel information. So we load up a taxi and go to the biggest hotel in town, the Bristol, where Cynthia has an emergency reservation (always prepared), to be used if she can't find something cheaper. Unload, the taxi driver waits to be paid, but the hotel won't change money at this hour. Bob is in no mood to be thwarted, makes rather a scene, and the desk clerk finally gives him some zlotys, he pays the cab driver and sends him on his way.

I continue as baggage monitor while C & B go to see about her reservation. No such thing. And no rooms available. The desk clerk phones around and sends us to the Saski Hotel. We eventually flag another taxi, load in all the bags, stumble in with the records, books, magazines, cameras, model airplane, coats, purse, etc. and roar off to the Saski, where we unload yet again onto the street and I stand yet again while C & B yet again go to check on rooms. I make quite a sight for the passing Poles.

After what seems like at least an hour and after I've memorized the wide streets and dimly lit buildings, and my arms are frozen into book-holding position (shades of UCLA finals week), and my spine is twisted into a permanent slump-must learn some yoga for such emergencies-they return. The room is flea-bitten, terrible, and they only have one. Cynthia has phoned the Embassy and they told her to go back to the Bristol. By now the streets are empty, it's getting very cold, and another 15 to 20 minutes go by before we see a taxi.

Same baggage scene, but frustration takes over and as we throw all the baggage in we do it less carefully, less efficiently, with end result we have less room for our bodies. (I now have Tolya's massive model airplane and most of the records on my squeezed in lap). Or maybe the taxis are getting smaller as the night wears on?

Back to the Bristol, unload. I retain my role as Bag Monitor. Is this how we are going to spend our 48 hours in Poland?

The Bristol still has no rooms; suggest we try the Grand. Right. Into another taxi-has the word gone round-"Hey, follow those dumb tourists, good business tonight!"? We should have kept the first one on a retaining basis.

Ever optimists, or tired, or plain stupid, we take everything out of the taxi for the-count'em, I've lost track-time. If the records aren't broken by now they should be.

But, they do have two rooms. For lots of zlotys (150). Question: Who cares? Answer: Bob. Quick conference: He's outnumbered, and figuring what a few more taxi rides will cost, this may turn out to be a bargain. Decision: Bath and Bed. Here and Now.

Wed. Aug. 19

Up early in our room with private bath. Strange that we live so luxuriously in communist countries. This is, we are told, the most modern hotel in Warsaw. Decor loud, not good, not too bad. Sort of second-class Hollywood & Vine. Not Moscow to be sure. Breakfast is served nicely by very pretty waitresses, (one for each of us) nicely uniformed, and the coffee and tea are pretty good.

Walk through Warsaw: After Moscow it looks like Paris. People are better dressed, women look like women again, there are cars, bikes, scooters, music, nightlife, the food looks better, quite a different world. However, there are still entire areas of the city that are completely leveled, and almost everywhere there are ruins, which make the few new buildings stand out like alien objects on an otherwise barren landscape.

The old city has been completely rebuilt. New bricks, old style, strange combination. We go through a department store, well stocked and people are buying. The bookstores have wonderful displays of book jackets and record covers with stunning graphic designs. Beautiful handmade textiles.

Bob makes his obligatory stop in the post-office, then we have ice-cream, pastry, and coffee. The next block offers a wine café-it is a very warm day, and it's pleasantly cool and dark inside, where we're served chilled glasses of white wine. Cynthia says that travel requires serious reevaluation of previous concepts regarding the order in which one consumes food. It's perfectly O.K. to have pastry and ice-cream as a first course. Flexibility is the key word, and the goal is to be fed whenever possible to keep up one's energy. Must remember to Make Note: Food Flexibility.

The Ghetto is a shattering experience. All that's left is a part of the watchtower, with its searchlights and barbed wire, and one wall of what used to be the community center, where there is a small memorial plaque. That's all. Except for racial memory. And pain.

Dinner in a cellar restaurant, Krokodyl. A small band, dancing, decent food and wine. We wander to the Bristol for coffee. Some of the Moscow crowd is there, and we sit and compare notes, everyone agreeing how much more "cosmopolitan" Warsaw is.

Back to our hotel to bathe, wash hair, write these notes and it's 4 AM before I get to bed. Obviously we have decided to stay on another day. The desk clerk assured us, as he would, of course, that we could stay two days on our visas. Taking the midnight train to Vienna tomorrow will get us to the border five hours after they have expired. We hope that our innocent American faces will get us by at that hour in the morning. Still, why are each of these decisions so agonizing to make?

Thurs. Aug. 20

Cynthia calls to wake us. Breakfast. American Embassy to chat with the people there. Do *they* think we'll have trouble overstaying our 48 hr. transit visa? They never like to commit themselves, but finally offer the following "It will depend on when we cross the border, but probably not." Cynthia, who had more foresight in Paris, has a five-day visa. She has to write an article or two and will meet us in Vienna.

Rest of the morning strolling: antique shops, art galleries, contemporary crafts, I buy a necklace made of "beads" of tightly wrapped patterned paper strung on a nylon cord. C & B go to the Press Club for lunch, I go back to the hotel to sleep, later pack up and check out of the room at 6. We three go to dinner at the Hotel Polanais. Not too clean. The waiter is fat and dirty which doesn't add to the ambience. There is a small noisy dance band and tiny dance floor, with mirror ball hanging from the ceiling. Good movie set.

As Cynthia and I go through the lobby, we're stopped by a man who says he is a journalist, could he interview us? We can't shake him so he follows us to our table. He introduces himself with a click of the heels and begins a monologue which lasts, with very minor and infrequent breaks, for over an hour. A cigarette dangles out of the side of his mouth, and when that's gone it is replaced with a matchstick. He speaks with great intensity, eyes squinting, and mouth spitting. In reality, and I question the use of such a word in talking about him, he is a fanatic from Afghanistan who wants to know if we're really interested in his cause because he needs representatives in the U.S.

I answer in all truth that his is "the best offer we've had all day."

One of the correspondents for a chain of Jewish papers, whom we had met in Moscow, joins us. Warsaw is "his city" and he is anxious to show us a few more things. He is visibly bored with our Afghanistan Connection who, as we get up to leave, corners Bob to ask again if he is really interested in his cause. Bob assures him he is. He insists: "And your wife and friend?" "Oh yes, they too." Then he asks Bob to lend him 25 zlotys to pay his hotel bill since he ran a little short this month. Bob sympathizes with him then explains that we're a bit short on cash too

We dash to the big Leonard Bernstein concert and go

backstage as the concert ends. We meet the U.S. Ambassador and his family, talk to the musicians who are packing up ready to leave tonight for Russia. We stand in line and congratulate Bernstein, tell him we hope there's still some caviar left in Moscow after our film festival.

We arrive at the train station one hour before departure, since there are no reservations in 2nd class. Why do so many trains in Europe leave at midnight? Very dramatic, but exhausting. We stand around again, tired and loaded down as always. Cynthia asks a crowd of touring French a few questions, but they can't confirm schedule. I'm beginning to dislike and distrust train travel in Europe, in spite of Agatha Christie.

Midnight: the train backs rapidly down the tracks, lurches forward, and crowds of people rush forward, run, climb, jump to get in, through the doors and windows, throwing their baggage in before them. Chaos reigns. We rush forward, carrying as much as we can, leaving the rest with Cynthia to watch, but I stop, horrified as I see a boy being dragged by the train. He can't hang onto the train and his suitcase at the same time, but if he lets go he'll be pulled under the train. I lose sight of him as he drops his bag to hang on with both hands, holding his legs up as you do when you grab onto a playground carousel's metal ring.

The train finally stops. We drag our heavy bags down to the last car, pushing and shoving and being pushed and shoved, throw what bags we can in through an open window, try to get on the train and make our way through the heaving humanity filling up the corridors and aisles, where everything is filled and jammed to bursting. Our bags have been kicked aside and back out into the corridor. The French seem to have taken over everything. My heart sinks, knowing we *must* take this train and get out of Poland before our visas expire.

Bob says with finality, "Well, that's it-we stand up for twelve hours, all the way to Vienna!" And I hate him for saying it. For once, I can't see any solution. He goes out to get the rest of the bags which Cynthia is holding for us. I'm glad we already made our arrangements to meet in Vienna I have visions of the train leaving without Bob, and just as he sets the bag and his foot on the step, the train does pull out.

It is so crowded there's hardly room to stand. The French move back and forth arranging themselves. One boy goes in and out of the toilet every few minutes. He has a cinder in his eye. Bob tells me to wait where I am while he tries to find something. I point out that even if I wanted to move I couldn't, that he will find me in the same spot when we pull into Vienna tomorrow.

He returns to say that the group of French Communist Youths who are returning from some conference or another are particularly rowdy and rough and everyone is scrambling around for some bit of territorial space in which to fit a knapsack on which to sit. But he found a locked compartment with some note in Polish tacked on the door, and maybe we can find a conductor or some official to open it up for us.

We inch our way through the car, thumping our bags on and over everyone rudely, unavoidably, until we get to the locked compartment. I try to figure out how "Quarantine" might look in Polish, but the compartment is dark and empty, a terrible, heartless, oversight in view of the sardine-can condition of the train.

Bob does not wait for a Samaritan conductor to appear. He takes out his fingernail file to unscrew a window pane. I'm worried, then amazed as within seconds what had been an unruly, surly, uncooperative crowd, to say the least, suddenly turns docile, and very helpful. Tools appear. The window is removed.

Bob reaches around, opens the door from the inside, and voila, we're seated and comfortable along with several of the French Communist kids, who arrange to take turns sitting. Next to us, and I really can't figure out where they came from is a large fully-bearded Franciscan monk in sackcloth and sandals, and a short, plump, sad-faced but smiling Pole with an Israeli passport. He explains that he only returned to Warsaw to visit his few remaining relatives. Most of his family, including his parents, wife, and children were killed during the war. He managed to escape to Israel.

We reach the border at 5 AM. An amazon of a Female-Hero-Polish-Border-Officer stomps into the compartment, flings on the lights, wakes us all up, and demands our passports. Second class travel is normally very cozy, but at this hour the bodies are piled thick and it takes some shuffling to get unraveled and dig out passports.

She does not wait patiently, and sweeps out in a self-righteous huff. The train is stopped in the darkness and time goes slowly, very slowly, each quarter hour increasing our anxiety quotient considerably. When she finally returns, over an hour later, she hands back all the passports except the one marked Israel. The poor man is obliged to open his battered suitcase, as she goes through every centimeter, tossing out his soiled underwear, unwrapping the newspaper packages his relatives had obviously given him, with bits of food and salamis, and most touching of all, a flannel-wrapped frame with a faded photograph of a family group, smiling faces, all of them.

The rest of us try not to watch, as the man stands by

helplessly watching all his possessions being thrown about, but as there is almost no room left in the compartment, and he can't hold everything in his arms, he is forced to pass some of the packages to us to hold for him.

When she is completely satisfied, about what I can't be sure-probably just that she has succeeded in humiliating him sufficiently, she hands him his passport, clumps out, and the train starts up soon after.

We try to help him put everything back, but in his haste, jamming everything in haphazardly, when he tries to close the suitcase, he breaks the handle. Bob and the monk find some string and manage to tie it together enough to shove back under the seat. We all share bits of food, pass our bottles of water around, and then settle down to try to get some more sleep.

Sometime later I wake up, look around and see that the Israeli has fallen asleep with his head on the monk's shoulders. Then I drift back to sleep as well.

20

Postcard from Vienna

Ãalter Hofkeller Zithermusik Spezialitaten
Historischer Tokayerkeller Des Kaisers

Train "transit" through Czechoslovakia, countryside quite beautiful, hope we can really visit someday. Finally arrive in Vienna, quite happy to leave inhumanly overcrowded train. Last sight as we left the station was the Israeli and the monk, leaving together, the monk helping the Israeli with his broken suitcase.

Very happy to be in the west again. The first thing we did was rush to the nearest newsstand for news from the "outside world."

Things we'll remember about Vienna: Reindeer steak with dark malt beer; weiner schnitzel; mountains of whipped cream, served individually on a plate or in a bowl; great feather beds; the crazy Hapsburgs and their palaces, and the Danube isn't blue.

Still Marveling,
C & B

21

Postcard #1 from Venice

Reproduction of engraving of San Marco
"Bucentaurus et Numdinae*f*
Venetae in die Ascensionis.....XIV"

Things really haven't changed much here, it seems, since "XIV", only the number of tourists and appearance of cameras. We're having great time taking pictures of tourists taking pictures.

Cynthia met us in Vienna in time for Wiener Schnitzel dinner with zitherist playing the Third Man Theme. I wondered if it were just for us or has Shubert been replaced indefinitely?

We all took yet another midnight train, to Milano-Venice with yet another heart stopping departure. Cynthia and I rushed onto the train to find seats while Bob dragged our heavier bags along the quay, and I lost sight of him as the train started to pull out. Note: no one blows a whistle, no one yells "All Aboard" or the equivalent; if there is a signal from someone somewhere, it is not communicated to anyone trying to get "All Aboard" at that last minute.

I started a frantic rush back through the coaches to try to find Bob, not knowing if he had managed to get on the train at the last moment. Crushing through the usual densely packed corridors, moving in desperate slow-motion, taking forever to work my way through car after car, my panic mounted as I realized I had our passports, money, tickets, just about everything Bob would need if he didn't get on this train in time. Alfred Hitchcock, take notes.

Just when I reached the last coach, I spotted Bob sauntering toward me, much too relaxed, much too calmly to match my cardiac arrest. Relief and anger! *Why didn't you walk faster?* (How could he, really?), *Weren't you worried? I have the passports, money, tickets?!!!* (Why should he have-<u>he</u> knew he was safely on the train?!)

Train Stressed,
Just C

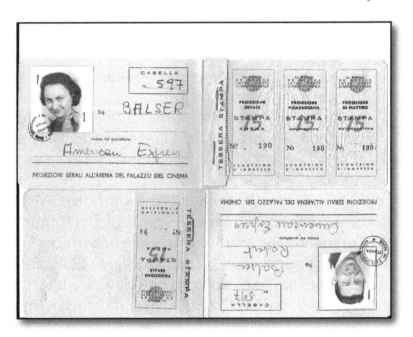

Venice press passes

Postcard #2 from Venice

I had barely recovered by the time we crossed the Italian border at 5 AM. Meanwhile, we are gradually picking up train travel techniques, i.e. the idea is not to sit <u>next</u> to your traveling companion, but across from each other, since it becomes more of a luxury to stretch your legs out and prop them on the seat across (you certainly can't stick your smelly feet in some stranger's face) than to find a place for your bobbing head. Of course, a place next to the window solves that problem, as well as giving you control of same, and use of small table underneath, and is to be sought after at all times.

Passing the beautiful Italian scenery, mountains, streams, cool mists over endless meadows, my recovery was complete, and in time to gather my forces for yet another train trauma. We had to change trains in Milano, not too difficult a maneuver as we were told we didn't even have to go into the station, the "local train to Venice" would be waiting on the tracks nearby.

As usual, no notice, no whistles, and by the time we got all our bags, hand luggage (Yes, I'm still carrying Tolya's albatross size model airplane) out on the tracks, spot what we thought was our train, got Cynthia on with part of our bags and went back for the rest, our throats aching as we struggled down the tracks, we watched the train Cynthia was on, with most of our bags, pull ever so slowly away from us and, almost dreamlike, disappear.

If I get spastic when I think of getting on or off a train, no wonder.

As we slumped our way into the station, we assumed

1) there was another train to Venice within the next few hours, 2) Cynthia would be willing and more important, able to, manage our bags, and not abandon them on the quay, and 3) she would somehow leave word where and how to find her/our bags.

TO BE CONTINUED...

Postcard #3

Ristorante Vida Pensione Lido Di Venezia

We did eventually get a train to Venice, where we found no sign of Cynthia. We changed money and took the first available motor launch along the Grand Canal then out onto the open sea to the Lido, where posters told us the film festival was taking place. Cynthia's husband, Richard, by chance, was hanging around the Press Office, and told us Cynthia was already at work. Were we glad to see him. He took us to their hotel to claim our bags (bless her strength and loyalty), and sat down to lunch with us in the outdoor garden under a very healthy, very green vine trellis. The pasta, wine, and talk completed our recovery, but I was the only one brave enough to order dessert. The waiter placed an enormous basket of fresh fruit in front of me, but all three of us, slowly, shamelessly, ate every last grapefruit-size peach, peach-size plum, plum-size grape, and, best of all, plump-size-fig. We were, of course, hungry for fresh fruit, and of course, had never seen such splendid specimens, but still...

I don't think the waiter believed it when he saw the bare basket, only a few fig leaves covering its nakedness. But he only charged us for one dessert, and gave me this free post-card.

Postcard #4

Silvana Mangano interprete del Film
La Grande Guerra

The Festival Office helped us find a room in Signorina Sorini's "Call me 'Elga'"'s apartment. She looks like Silvana Mangano, very high heels clicking at all hours across the shiny tile floors. She adores film, rushes out to the showings, usually accompanied by an assortment of rather attractive male companions, (Aside: Lord, Italian men really are handsome.)

The apartment is stark, with long, cold corridors, but attractive. and our room is nice enough. We think the mattresses and pillows are stuffed with straw-they smell good and feel crunchy. One drawback is the annual shortage of water on the Lido in summer-*tutti turisti and all that*-and in order to conserve what little they have, the water in her block is turned off all morning, every day.

Camping was very good training for the rich life on the luxurious Lido!

Ever Enchanted,
C & B

22

The Venice Film Festival

Two weeks in Venice, basking in the sun of the Lido by day, films, receptions, movie stars, glamour, free food at night, what a racket!

Once settled in our room Chez Elga, we plunged into the festival routine once again. Our credentials were ready, but somehow someone, probably due to confusing our mailing address with our employer, had us registered as representing American Express. Well, it sounds as if it <u>could</u> be a newspaper. But as long as we have our press passes to the showings, and lots of invitations to freebie receptions and cocktail parties...

The routine here includes fairly early risings, a dash out to the nearest bar (no water in the house, remember) for morning coffee, which is not really a large cup of hot beverage as we know it. The first time we ordered "due cafes" and received tiny cups with barely a thimbleful of thick brown colored syrup, we thought we had ordered wrong. No. That's what the Italians call coffee. They toss it back in one gulp. Next we ordered "due tostis", then watched a long procedure in which the waiter very carefully cut and trimmed four pieces of bread, searched for ham, then cheese, which he also carefully cut and trimmed to match the bread slices. Once constructed, he put them onto a grill, and while they were "tosting", dashed into the kitchen to return with two small trays, knives, forks, and tissue-thin napkins. Result: two elaborate toasted ham and cheese sandwiches, exactly what Bob didn't want to stand, wait, and worse, pay for, and exactly what I didn't want to ask my aching stomach to process which was still trying to deal with my share of yesterday's giant basket of fruit.

We soon found the best bet was to head for the nearby Festival Mostra bar, where we could get crossantes and "cappuchino": <u>two</u> thimbles of coffee syrup in a bigger cup filled up with hot frothy milk. Once, at a Press Film Promotion Breakfast at the very fancy Dardinelli Hotel, we even got eggs, some treat. I quickly missed all that Russian caviar and kafir every morning.

Depending on how often we could escape the film schedule, we spent mornings on the beach, or dashed over to Venice to fall faint with wonder in front of all that architectural glory. Not really detracting from the real spirit of Venice, the masses of tourists, by day, seem quite content congregating in the Piazza di San Marco, where they can feed the overstuffed pigeons, see and be seen. And at night it's so dark in those tiny narrow alley-like streets and canals you don't see them floating to and fro on their 3,000 lire-per-hour gondola rides.

No, we did not take a gondola-too expensive. We, fresh from the Soviet Union, took the working people's vaporettos, the large, bus-like motor launches which travel the Grand Canal, stopping at piers instead of street corners.

It was hard to juggle all the official and unofficial receptions, cocktails, promotions, press conferences, with the actual screenings, which start at 9AM and go on all day and night. We had passes for the official evening 9:30 show in the outdoor arena, which didn't require formal dress. It was also a bit noisier there and not so embarrassing when we nodded, often slept, and occasionally snored during the films. Even if we were fluent in the languages of most of the films, which we are not, the Italian subtitles weren't very helpful. But even worse were the simultaneous translations in English which very poor actors and not very competent translators speak their version of the dialogue over the sound track, making it impossible to hear/understand either one, droning such emotional lines as "I love you but I must kill you" in a concentrated monotone which all things considered is probably better not heard....)

Mostly though, we were by then suffering severely from sleep deprivation. You must remember that since we left Stockholm, my average bedtime has been 4:30 AM. Like I said, European trains all seem to leave at midnight, and second class travel doesn't provide the ultimate in sleeping facilities. In fact, most of the time it doesn't provide more than a hard sit and, if you're lucky, a friendly and/or just as tired shoulder on which to lean.

When we got to Moscow, I was so hyperstimulated most of the time that even if we got in at two in the morning, I'd sit down and start to write notes in my Dagbok, or address a few dozen more of the seemingly hundreds of postcards we were sending back home. I also spent two nights after 2 AM writing the article for A.P., since those were the only quiet moments I had in which to work. Finally, when we knew we were going to Poland I started reading all of Cynthia's background material. I knew so little and somehow when you're in or at a place it suddenly becomes the most vital spot in the world and you want to know everything about it. Bob, however, being a stamp collector, astounds me constantly by knowing the correct name, spelling, and geographical location, as well as of much of the history-especially the heroes and battles-of wherever we are.

Finally, after all the reading and writing was done, I'd go into the bathroom, see our own private bathtub-the first since we left home, and absolutely couldn't let it go to waste. Voila, hot bath around 3:30. And so it went.

But Venice is even worse. The movies begin late, both to accommodate local dinner hour, as well as the setting sun, for those attending the outdoor screenings. Afterwards everyone wanders over to the Excelsior to discuss the films and be seen. When Cynthia's festival hospitality ran out she and Richard moved into Elga's, in the room next door to ours, and when we finally walk home together, well after three each morning, Cynthia and Bob wisely conk out while I am left to listen to Richard, who is used to being alone all day writing his novel, so that when he finally gets hold of somebody, usually at night, he bends ears until they drop from exhaustion. Here I am the chosen one, and as conversations go, these are some of the finest. He can converse brilliantly, easily, knowledgably on everything from films to furniture, if only they didn't go on until sunrise, when the first screening sometimes begins at nine...I could appreciate them much, much more.

Re: food, Cynthia was right. We pay for breakfast cappuccino, and from then on it's receptions and cocktails and occasionally a full blown sit-down dinner. She and Bob are getting to be like old pros in getting invitations, or looking as if we have them, sweeping past rigid doormen with such aplomb that we are rarely stopped and questioned.

The producers and production companies are in mortal hospitality combat. There is the United Artists Free Bar on the beach (lots of Cinzano), DiLaurenti's cocktail at the

Excelsior, the official Spanish film was terrible, but their reception was 4 star, a full feast of Spanish specialties. The very top of the line was the French Reception in the Ducal Palace in Venice. We took a speed boat over the lagoon, and were dropped off in front of the plush carpet leading to the lobby and the wide marbled staircase posted with men in bright orange, white, and black costumes, holding apparently very heavy candelabras, all aglow, swaying slightly, either from the weight, or the chamber music ensemble in the background playing Vivaldi.

The reception itself took place on an enormous balcony overlooking a green and blue illuminated interior courtyard on one side, San Marco on another, with the lagoon and the yellow lights of the Lido in the background. The tables and tables of food offered everything from caviar to cream tarts, along with the best of French champagne. Richard has a totally different Eats Theory, and was only too happy to explain that at such events he always has his "fish course first", digging right into the caviar, smoked salmon, tiny baby squid marinated in oil, clams, moules au Provencal, shrimp, and lobster tidbits. Only then does he turn his attention to the various lamb, beef, veal, and pork dishes. This is followed by judicious selections of salads and vegetables, and much later dozens of desserts. Cynthia, of course, went her own way, and as we started to follow Richard dutifully around the course, she immediately plunged into the strawberry gelati, and moved off in the opposite direction.

Once we were completely stuffed and could ignore the endless stream of waiters bringing in more and more trays of delicacies, we could turn our attention to finding familiar faces and discuss the films of the day, finding yet again great diversity of opinion. *Sight and Sound,* the soundest critic; *Variety*, more interested in Box Office; the French and Finnish journalists particularly picky for some reason, all very interesting discussions. The producers tend to be generous or non-committal, hoping, I guess, to get the same treatment for their offerings. Exception: Rosselini, with his new De Sica film, which isn't one of their best.

Lionel Rogasin is here with his recently completed *Come Back Africa*. He has brought along the star, Miriam Makeba, whom he thinks will become A Big Singer in Europe and the U.S. She is beautiful and charming and we sit listening to her, enthralled with her "clicking" demonstrations. Joe Strick is presenting "The Savage Eye", and we hope it's a winner.

We met John and Faith Hubley and their children. They're presenting "Moonbird" in competition, art work and voices by the kids. John is the hero of all us Animation folk. What a thrill to sit on the beach together exchanging travel anecdotes! They too, always arrive home from their trips broke, and have to ask their doorman for money to pay the taxi. We tell them Bob's father has already warned us that he is not going to wire us money to get home "Ever Again." (Note: we have not mentioned in any of our communiques home that we only have two traveler's checks left.... Note 2: It is extremely fortunate our funds are lower than low. If not they would surely fall victim to the temptations on every corner, and have us trying to find room in the trunk of the car, already packed with camping gear and the wooden shoes from Holland, for dozens of dazzling examples of Venetian beads and Murano glass baubles.)

We now realize that if one were sturdy enough, with a hale and hearty digestive system, one could conceivably start out on January 1st, and attend one or another film festival straight through December 31st. We have even heard complaints from some conscientious film critics that festival planners do not leave enough travel time between festival openings and closings. One hears such jewels: "You weren't in Cracow?" "How could I when I had to cover Locarno."

That evening, as the film started in the Arena, it began to rain. What started out as a sprinkle, soon developed into a downpour, sending everyone screeching and scurrying to get out and under cover. With much turmoil and silent-movie crashing about, the attendants tried to put up some kind of canvas cover, but only succeeded in channeling the rain into more forceful waterfalls, unfortunately, right where most of us huddled waiting. Eventually the loudspeakers announced that the show for the evening was most definitely over and attempts would be made to reschedule the film the following day.

Soaked, we headed back to Elga's, with Elga, who somehow in the short walk managed to pick up a couple of rather interesting looking men, one of whom was a Jewish dentist from Paris who started to tell us WW II stories. When we got home she rushed in to change her clothes, Bob grabbed his bow-tie, and before I really realized what the plan was they all flew out to try to get into the main screening.

All I wanted was a bath. There was running water at that hour. However, for several days there had been trouble with the hot water, and we had been making do with cold, very cold showers. But now I was damned if I was going to get into a cold shower, I had just had one outside. And so it was that in glorious Venice, in the middle of August, in a somewhat elegant apartment, I found myself all alone, carrying pot after pot of boiling water down the long hallway from kitchen to bathroom, hoping to eventually get a short lukewarm soak.

Scene in one of the local restaurants: a pair of journalists, those of lower-than-low budgets, told us they had
found an excellent, inexpensive trattoria, and were only too
happy to share it with us. We all sat at a long table, work-
men eaters and family waiters shouting, with Mama in the
kitchen stirring cauldrons and screaming back at the rest
of the family slinging platters of great smelling and tasting
food. One goes back to the open kitchen to see what is cooking. One makes one's choice, and after much discussion
(or pointing) and with more yelling back and forth, one is
eventually served. In addition to all the people, there were
several cats prowling the premises, and a very cute puppy
dog drinking out of the bucket in which the lettuce was
being "washed." I think the French call it "ambiance." Our
health inspectors would turn to stone, but the food was
sure great and I'm still here to write about it.

Finally, the last night of the Festival. Bob spent most
of the day running back and forth to the press office trying to get tickets for the gala closing ceremony and film,
in the main theater. The P.R. in charge was frazzled by
the crowds pushing and shoving wanting exactly the same
thing. Persistent as always, Bob managed to shove himself
up to the first row, and I guess that after telling him to come
back so many times, the P.R. guy began either to feel sorry
for him or simply wanted to get rid of him. He told Bob to
wait while he tried to disperse the latest crowd of seekers,
one of whom was a late arrival from *TIME*. With a wave of
desperation the guy behind the counter looked straight at
the man from *TIME* and pointing to Bob said, "Look, here
is the reporter from *AMERICAN EXPRESS*! And I can't even
find a ticket for him!!!!!

Soon after the coast cleared somewhat, the man reached
under the counter and palmed Bob a small envelope with

one ticket "for your wife"...assuming that representing such an important paper as *AMERICAN EXPRESS*, Bob already had his priority press pass, which, of course he did not. But good old Cynthia, pro that she is, took us, me, brides-maid dressed, and told bow-tied Bob to hang around out-side, as she went in on her photographer's pass, Richard on her ticket, I with the extra ticket, courtesy of *AMERICAN EXPRESS*. She got us all seated, then returned to bring Bob in on Richard's ticket.

The film was "Some Like It Hot" - marvelous!, the cer-emonies were lengthy but glamorous, and the midnight supper on the 2nd floor of the Excelsior was sumptuous, fol-lowed by a splendid fashion show and a jazz session down-stairs, champagne flowing throughout.

As we headed for home at 5 AM I wondered at the stamina these film festival folk have, and reminded my-self to ask them for their favorite, most effective hang-over remedies.

We lingered a few more days for more intensive sight-seeing in Venice. We had given Tintoretto short shrift, indeed, and a bit more Lido beach time. Cynthia and Richard guided us to yet another truly thrilling evening, telling us that "These things are usually expensive, but if one hangs around until the last minute, one can often get reduced tickets." So we waited for half-price, and entered the courtyard of a wonderful old palace, with amber lights illuminating the garden sculpture. We sat on silk covered violin-backed chairs and listened to a Monteverdi (Richard pointed out the literal translation of the name: Greenberg) concert, with harpsichord, accompanied by a rather dra-matic male-female fencing ballet duo.

The following days, as the giant promotion posters started coming down, the temporary festival installations dismantled, and most of the producers, directors, stars, journalists, critics, and hangers-on long gone, the skies turned grey, a rather cold wind blew up, and on September 9th, as we too packed up, it definitely felt as if summer was over, time to get back to Stockholm, pick up our car, and Make Decisions.

Full-up
C & B

23

Venice - Stockholm

We do not move with grace. The morning we were all to leave Venice, Cynthia, efficient as always, had the train schedule to Milano, and the decision was made to get the 12:52 *noon*, not midnight train, for a change.

But as the morning went on, the packing became more intense. One picks up much bulk at these festivals, and we dare not toss any of it until we have written our reviews and articles for *FILM* QUARTERLY, although as we are beginning to realize, it is rather difficult to provide in-depth analysis of plot intricacies in "foreign films" shown with subtitles neither of us understands.

C & R seemed to be having similar packing problems, and as we dashed in and out of each other's open doors-should we? CAN we make it? Yes, No, Yes.

We ended up running, bags flapping (don't ever forget Tolya's plane) to the Excelsior, threw everything into a waiting motorboat and had a perfectly good excuse to take a last plush, dashing, private, express ride across the lagoon, arriving in a splash of speed and spray at the train station for another teeth-clenching dash aboard the 12:52 as it pulled away.

Bereft of proper provisions, we happily finished off Richard's freebie vermouth, leaving a pile of empty miniatures by the time we arrived in Milano at 4:30. It wasn't too tough to decide to spend the night there, in a "reasonable pensione." Lots to see. One can scramble around the Duoma's roof, and see all that Gothic wonder in close-up. So *THAT'S* what all those spires look like! How come they made them so detailed and varied way up here when no one down there would be able to tell a sculptured pineapple from a sculptured pear?

The next morning C & R got us up at 9 to say goodbye. They were off to Rapallo to visit their "Rich Milanese Friends." This tearfully ended a month's journey together. Cynthia gave me a tiny nosegay which produced yet another tear or two. We promised to keep in touch.

Great day in Milano, the Brera Gallery, lunch at La Scala Ristoranti, across from the Opera House, and more adventures gathering supplies for the 36-hour train-boat trip ahead. We managed to get cheese, salami, hard-boiled eggs, bread, Motta Panetone, tomatoes, fruit, water, vermouth, chianti, chocolate, everything but salt for the eggs and tomatoes. Nowhere to be found, not in *la salumeria, la macelleria, la latteria, la pescheria, il supermercato, la panetteria, la pasticceria, il grande magazzino, la drogheria, it negozio di frutta e verdure, il negozio di liquori, la farmacia...* We asked, of course, and we thought our *"Dove posso trovare del sale"* rather well done, but nobody seemed to understand us. Several kept saying *"la tabacceria"*, and we thought maybe they thought we were asking for a special brand of cigarettes.

I was willing to give up, especially since, as the afternoon wore on, I was already in the throes of Pre-Train Boarding Trauma, and in need of a strong support group, not a Salt Quest. But Bob would not think of embarking on such a journey without salt for his eggs and tomatoes.

Any longer and I might have started to froth, when we passed a tobacco shop and, by chance, I glanced in the window, and saw a package of salt. Who's to think that, like tobacco, salt is a state monopoly, and one can only buy it in state controlled tobacco shops? They all *tried* to tell us, "*LA TABACCHERIA!*"

We ran to catch the 5:32 for Stockholm, and it took several hours of looking out the window at the beautiful lake country as the lights went on in the mountains, to calm down. It gets dark early now, around 7, which makes me sad, I don't want this particular summer to end. But if it hadn't got dark I think we would have been seriously tempted to get off the train and linger by those exquisite lakes.

We had several changes of compartment companions. Most of the tourists seem to have gone home, leaving at least the corridors passable. Three English girls giggled non-stop until they got off in Basel. They were replaced by two very large, very loud German ladies with one dog. "*Mutti, Mutti, Mutti, gahen en heren!*" With great effort they got themselves settled until the conductor asked them for their ticket for "das schwinehundt", which created yet another noisy scurry and tossing about of most of their numerous belongings.

Once that was arranged things finally quieted down until 3:30 AM when shrieks filled the compartment. "*MUTTI, MUTTI, IS DAS FRANCFORT? ACH! SCHNELL! MINE HUNDT! SCHNELL! DANKESCHEIN! SCHNELL!* And we could hear them still screaming on the platform as the train pulled away.

We woke up at 8:30 in Hanover, and made the mistake

of ordering coffee to have with our picnic breakfast. $1.50. We forgot coffee is expensive in Germany.

More beautiful scenery, reading and writing, chatting a bit with latest compartment companions, a Swedish couple who were enthralled with paintings they had bought in Milano, six large oils for $60. Ever thankful we have no storage room in the Peugeot we congratulated them on their purchases.

We had our picnic lunch which was the same as our picnic breakfast only with a bit more cheese, before the train boarded the Grosenberg-Gedser ferry, giving us a chance to go on deck for a nice three-hour boat ride in the sun.

We had our picnic dinner, which was the same as our picnic breakfast and picnic lunch, just before we arrived in Copenhagen at 8:30. We unloaded, I reverted to my post as bag-watcher-monitor, while Bob went to mail the postcards and buy some good Danish smorrebrod.

We boarded the 9:30 sleeper to Stockholm to great confusion. The Sleeper Captain complained, "Those Boat People just don't know how to sell tickets!" They apparently not only had sold my berth twice, they had assigned me to an all-male compartment. I had to move in with two Italian ladies, one with a baby. Never mind, there were clean sheets and a chance to be horizontal again.

Every once in awhile during the night I was aware of clanging train stopping, changing tracks, loading and unloading itself on and out of boats, and it took me five minutes to wake up when the conductor wanted my ticket in the middle of the night. Barbaric.

There was no chance, however, of my "sleeping in", since the Italian ladies were up at the crack of 7, arranging themselves, the child, and all their equipment.

It is a bright, clear, sunny day, and we pass tiny towns

full of colored gardens, half in sun, half in shade. With the window open, I see and smell the trees, woods, forests. What a beautiful country is Sweden.

It becomes crisp and cool as Bob joins me for our picnic breakfast, with good fresh, hot Swedish coffee, which thankfully isn't as expensive as German coffee. In fact we're congratulating ourselves-only $5.00 for our two sleepers last night, and it has turned out to be a good trip after all, not too tiring, not too dirty, and not too expensive.

We're due to arrive in Stockholm at 9:00 AM, and I'll mail this from there. I think we still have enough money for stamps...

Love, a kilo for every kilometer,
C & B

24

Copenhagen (Laterna Film)

October 1, 1959

Here I sit, in one ugly room: one wall maroon, three walls green, with our little camp table and 1-burner Gaz stove set up in the corner next to the wash basin. I stare at a plate hanging on the maroon wall, covering a hole, (I checked) with the inscription, in English yet, "How Doth The Little Busy Bee...Improve Each Shining Hour...And Gather Honey All The Day...From Every Opening Flower..."

But I Digress.

When we got back to Stockholm, I waited as usual, in the station with the bags, while Bob went to get the car out of storage, hoping there would be enough money left to pay for a hotel. When he returned he was ecstatic-we'd left it so long they charged us the monthly, not the daily rate. Total: $12! With that we totaled the money we had left, $25, including all loose change.

So we could afford to seek and find a very inexpensive hotel. Note: camping season definitely ends end of August. We piled all our newly acquired bulk into the back seat and went directly to American Express to pick up the mail. Dozens of letters, and telegrams from Laterna Film in Copenhagen: "Contact Us Immediately-Urgent!!!"

Bob phoned, and it seemed as if, on the basis of his very vague letter telling them we thought we might be back in Copenhagen around August 20th, Mogens Skot-Hansen, the owner of the studio, committed Laterna Film-and Bob- to deliver a 10-minute animated film to for the Kul Koks industry (it means coke and cinders, but it is funny to see KUL KOKS in red neon all over Copenhagen...) by October 20th! And this was already the middle of September (!)

Bob covered up the receiver, looked at me and asked, "They want me to do a film right away, what shall I say?"

I motioned frantically to the pitiful pile of kroner-"Say 'Yes'!" At the same time I wondered if we had enough money for the gas and ferry fare needed to get us to Copenhagen.

Then two things happened. We went back to the travel agency to try to get a refund on the unused Russian "days" and trains (the Moscow-Stockholm train/boat return). We were told we'll have to wait on the train refund, as tickets have to be sent to Russia, (read never-never land,) but we did get a refund on the "days". We were on a roll! Even with the 15% refund charge of $7, we got $45 back for the "days."

Next, we were driving around trying to find a really cheap hotel when we heard a terrible scraping sound on the right side of the car. Someone had opened up a truck door just as we were going by, making a major mess of his door and a minor mess of ours. I managed to open and close my door, barely.

The driver apologized, in perfect English, and as I babbled nervously about how we were in a hurry and had to leave Stockholm immediately, he calmly gave us his card, suggested that since we could use the door, we simply get an estimate for the repairs, he would give us the money, and we could have the door straightened out at our convenience.

We dashed to the nearest garage, they clicked their tongues a bit, looked at the car door, and gave us an official estimate. We took it back to the address on the card, a very elegant building, and tried not to look too shabby as we asked for Mr. Jorgansen, who turned out to be the director of what was one of the big fur companies in Stockholm. He smiled warmly, apologized again, said he rarely drove any of their trucks, wrote out a check for the equivalent of $35, and wished us "Godt Reiser."

We were rich!

So we detoured to Oslo.

But not before we phoned the Swedish friends we had met before. They invited us to their country home that evening, where we delivered our Russian Report, showed them our slides and Dima's paintings, drank Algerian wine, with cheese, honey, toast, sweets and coffee, and as we were leaving they handed us a small metal match-box holder with the inscription: "The World Is A Book And He Who Stays At Home Reads Only One Page."

Another tough good-bye, and promises to Keep In Touch.

We stayed just long enough the next day to listen to the last outdoor concert of the year at the Kungsgarten, take photos of Herman Miller furniture in the NK department store, and then on to Oslo. I know we promised Skot-Hansen we would get right to Copenhagen, but we did have a pocketful of kroner again, and it *was* just "sort of" out of the way, and it would be pleasant to visit that nice couple we met in the Brussels campground, and after all, we had never been to Norway...

The drive to Oslo was beautiful, and we *only* stopped

to see a tiny church, but, well, we had wanted to see a special museum with complete firefighting equipment, and when we couldn't find the museum Bob went to the Police Station, and returned to the car with a police escort, who drove to the Fire Station where the chief found the key, hopped into a spare fire wagon, and led us through town to the special collection housed in an old wooden building. We chatted, took photos, thanked them profusely for their time, left our police-fire truck escort and moved on.

At the border there were very confusing road signs trying to tell us to shift to left hand drive again. Once on the "right side of the road", we chased a particularly spectacular sunset, with the full moon coming through a cloud ring behind us, until we found a Mission Hotel, which are always nice, clean, and very inexpensive. However, this time we were shuffled right through the Hotel, into the Bible School, which is also used as a hotel when the students are busy praying elsewhere, and our room was even colder and more austere than all the other Spartan "rum"s we were usually offered. How we miss the double sleeping bag of old.

Our Belgian campground friends invited us to breakfast. We thought that was very sweet of them, and expected the normal European crust of bread and cup of coffee. No one told us they're big on breakfasts in Norway. They started their day and ours with several varieties of fish, many choices of cheese, scrambled eggs and hard-boiled eggs, cold meats, tomatoes, rolls, crackers, home-made wheat bread, slabs of bright yellow butter, homemade strawberry jam, big glasses of fresh milk and endless cups of hot steaming coffee with rich, thick cream. I kept wanting to ask what they had for lunch and dinner and why?

A quick look at the Oslo fiord-everything is so sharp and

bright in these northern cities it fools me into thinking I can throw away my glasses. The Viking Ship Museum with the Kon Tiki, and a *very* quick purchase of a pair of real Lap sealskin bedroom slippers, (actually, it might have been better if I hadn't-boy do they smell-we have to catch our breath every time we open the trunk), and ever conscientious, we made our way back to Sweden and Copenhagen.

For hours before we reached Copenhagen we indulged in variations of the following dialogue: "How much do you think Skot-Hansen is going to offer me to do this film?"

"Well, how long will it take to do it?"

"That's not the point. It's an 8 to 10 minute film and normally would take a couple of months. But if he has a deadline of October 20th and today is already September 18th..."

"Well, he <u>has</u> to give me at least a few hundred dollars"

"Unless he has a tight budget."

"Depends on how expensive apartments are, if we're going to be here a month we'll have to find an apartment."

"We can probably expect $300."

"$200 surely..."

And so it went as we pulled up in front of Laterna Film in the middle of Copenhagen, noting it was quite a bit colder and definitely windier than when we were here in July.

Skot-Hansen was very relieved to see us at last, welcomed us warmly into his office, furnished with all that splendid teak and black leather, offered us coffee served in those charming blue and white porcelain cups, and got right down to business.

The film: who, what, where, why, and most important, when: October 20th very definite deadline. Style, sound track, final recording dates were all discussed.

The studio was full up with crews working on a feature film with local stars, but they would help us find an apartment with space for Bob to work there. However, the housing shortage is severe and it wasn't going to be easy.

No mention of money, and everything was so cheery and straightforward *I* certainly didn't want to bring it up.

More talk about supplies, camera facilities, etc. etc. We made an appointment for the next morning to meet several people who would be Bob's special assistants, and someone to help me find an apartment, and we all stood up.

It was then, as we were dusting off the cookie crumbs, and putting on our coats that Skot-Hansen slapped his forehead and said, "Oh, yes, money...would $1,000 for the job be satisfactory?"

I almost choked, Bob cleared his throat several times before he could mumble, trying very hard to be casual, "Oh, yes. Sure."

!!!That was more than half our budget for six whole months in Yerp!!!

Aside: Figure we left L.A. April 1st, although we didn't arrive in France until the 24th, and this was September 18 and we still had a few dollars left, not enough, certainly, for tickets home, but that was never really in the budget, don't tell Dad. So we almost made our six month goal. (You figure it out, Frommer, did we make it on $5 A Day?)

Next, back up those 96 steps to Fru Fishers who kept us in sherry, cookies and great breakfasts ("let me do your laundry, no extra charge"), and even better news for our Mission Hotel broken backs, she had just purchased new mattresses to go with those keen feather quilts.

She simply couldn't understand why we were going to look for an apartment instead of just staying on with her- weren't we comfortable? Maybe she should get in a few more varieties of honey for our breakfasts? Would I like to cook some meals with her? (I did and "our" carrot pudding and kidney stew were terrific. However, I later gave up on orange marmalade when I saw the five pages of tightly handwritten instructions).

She even offered to clear away the stacks of her late husband's paintings, the shawl covered tables and overstuffed chairs in the front parlor, for a place for Bob to work.

We tried to explain as clearly and kindly as we could that we really did need more than a bedroom and shared bathroom for the time we expected to be in Copenhagen. And no matter where we moved we would continue to see each other, (undaunted by those 96 steps, which she, by the way, continues to run up and down countless times during the day, which may explain her hearty state of health).

However, after too many days of frustrated searching in which we did not find a splendid, medium sized apartment (we weren't greedy!), furnished with lovely teak furniture-the sort of place we had had in mind-we settled for two rooms, not adjoining, in a private home. The family occupies the ground floor, and the second floor has been converted into a Pension, with five rooms and one bathroom. There are hot plates set up in the basement for cooking.

We asked for and were granted permission to set up and use our 1-burner Gaz stove in the room, found that the tiny space between the French doors and the railing overlooking the garden was big enough, just, and certainly cold enough, to keep a liter of milk, bit of butter and cheese from spoiling.

So we're basically back to camping again. Indoors. Oh well, it's cheap and within walking distance of Centrum.

We gave Fru Fisher a very vague description of our new quarters, and made no promises to have her over for tea. She would never understand our preferring these two rooms to her two rooms, and we doubt we could explain that here we have, if not much else, more privacy, and although rather primitive, our own cooking facilities. She has been so absolutely sweet to us we certainly didn't want to hurt her feelings. We'll invite her *out* to tea as soon as we can.

Now while Bob whiles away the time whipping out the film in the room across the public, not private, hall, I've unloaded all our junk and am making a fairly valiant effort to get organized, something we've been threatening to do since the day we left home. Laundry into the Quik Vask, coats and sweaters to the Rensning-Farvning place, films processed, just like that "Little Busy Bee..."

I have no idea how long we'll be here. There is such an impossible deadline on this film Bob is doing that he is working day and night and there hasn't been any time to discuss future plans. Anyhow, if we stick to our Mission Hotel budget, we figure the money we get from this work will finance another two to three months' travel.

Knowing this does not, however, stop the recurring nightmares I've been having, where I dream we're back in L.A., and I'm moaning, "Why are we *here* when there are so many things we haven't seen yet in Europe?" I wake up in a cold sweat, open the French doors a teeny bit more, almost freeze doing it, convincing myself that we are, indeed, still in Denmark, definitely not in Southern California.

Love to all you homebodies,
C & B

25

Copenhagen

Big news, and I'm sure you'll rejoice with me when I tell you that Mark, my former hairdresser, (also my travel guru, as you'll remember), now resides in Copenhagen. He lives in a gorgeous apartment with two great Danish guys. We've had happy reunion, hair-dos galore, strongly under the influence of Danish Akavit (Snaps), which tastes like Anisette and makes Bourbon seem like cough medicine. No photos please. And just as soon as Bob is available they have appointed themselves our Official Tour Guides. Besides sumptuous dinners in their this-is-what-I-expected-ALL-Danish-apartments-to-look-like, they are already planning long lunches out in the country with full day excursions thereabouts.

Meanwhile, while Bob works, I'm discovering why the early name for this city was Kopmannahan, "Merchants Haven." A veritable shopper's paradise. We do have a bit more money, lots of birthday and anniversary presents are long overdue, and everything is so inexpensive-a fatal combination.

Silver, ceramics, glassware, textiles, baskets, handcrafts, jewelry, (I've discovered amber), it's very hard to pull me off the Stroget, Copenhagen's Bond Street, Fifth Avenue, and Rodeo Drive, all rolled into a series of streets in Centrum, and into museums where one sees the same beautiful things, only older and not for sale.

I can't even count on exhaustion to slow me down. Everything seems to be within easy walking distance, and right in the middle of the Stroget is the Jordbaerkellren (Strawberry Celler), where I can try to order, if I can catch the eye of any one of several wonderful ladies who may not, but certainly act as if they have owned the place for centuries. It's their private world you've wandered into, and they're definitely in charge down there. But it's worth all the waiting and fussing when they finally set your tray on the table and sing out, "Vaer saa god..." ("There you have it...") with the most scrumptious fresh fruit "malts" or salads, with or without yogurt, to be dowsed with fine crumbs of rugbrod (pumpernickel) and brown sugar from bowls on every table. If you have room after all that, their tiny cups of freshly roasted coffee with a selection of small pastries will only add another three kroner (50 cents) to the bill.

When everything closes up around me at 5:30, I can either take the long walk or short trolley ride home and tell Bob what a tiring afternoon I've had...

Note: The Danes have a serious Thanking Obsession. "Tak", pronounced "tack" means "thanks," and strict protocol requires at least one, preferably two, or as many as time allows, for –underline-everything.

When one leaves friends one "taks" for the drinks, food, and evening separately, and when one meets again the next time, the first thing said must be "Tak for sidst" "Thanks for the last time."

One "taks" when one asks a question and again when one replies.

Conversation between Bob and me at the table now goes something like this: "Bread, tak? Tak tak. Please hand me the smor (butter), tak, tak, tak. And the knife. Tak for knife. Tak, tak. Tick-tak. Tak-tock. Tick-tak-toe-tak. Tak tak. –underline- Toosund tak (Thousand thanks)

Admittedly, it carries politeness to a fine art, but it certainly puts a big pressure on us, culture wise. Tak for denne gang! ("Thanks for this time")

C & B

26

Copenhagen Film Finished

Tuesday, October 20

The Big Day

Bob finished the film on time and still had strength to go to the official screening this morning. He could hardly believe the applause, the laughter, and congratulations! I could, he turned out a really good 8 1/2 minute film, in less than a month, a bit of a miracle even with "working 24 hours a day and all night too."

As we stood around accepting accolades, Skot started talking about our "future in Copenhagen." He has several animated films he wants to do and obviously Bob is his man.

Later Bob had his usual post-film depression and, face drawn, told me in all seriousness, that he "simply must learn to roll with success..."

By that time I was rolling with plans: look again for a real apartment, you can't imagine the trouble I have trying to replace our small butane tank. Who uses camping gaz in the middle of winter? Make new, longer lists of all the great museums, excursions, shops, restaurants, we haven't yet seen/done. Remind myself to send a note to that nice Finnish producer to explain why we didn't stop in Helsinki to visit his studio.

And how nice it will be not to pack and unpack-usually with dirty laundry-for a while.

Who wants to travel at this time of year anyhow?

Come to think of it, this *IS* travel...

Will advise.

Excitedly,
C & B

Drawing of Bob and Cima shopping in Copenhagen

Acknowledgements

Without our cousins, Anne Legge and Eli Balser, this book couldn't have been published. Both Anne and Eli are excellent artists, published authors, and like Bob, professional animators. Anne found the Simon and Schuster/Archway Publishing web site and set up my first telephone conversation with Virginia Morrel. Eli has been at my side, scanning, formatting, and preparing the manuscript for submission.

Bryan Di Salvatori, who not only encouraged me, but painstakingly and enthusiastically edited my long neglected manuscript, and gave me the courage to **DELETE.**

To my sister, Renee, who saved every single letter, postcard, photo, and crazy stuff, like bus tickets, theater stubs, and advertisements for funny soft drinks we sent her, and returned it all back to me to be included here.

To our son, Trevel, who has brought us the kind of joy we didn't even know existed, and now with his wife, Patricia, and their family, it continues to grow with their help and support.

To our parents, now gone, who reluctantly let us go, and aside from constant nagging: "When are you coming back home?" finally realized our "home" was in Europe.

To all the friends and friends of friends who read these barely readable onion-skin copies, and kept encouraging me all these years, to "Put these letters in a book!"

Last but not least, Heather Perry, who so very quickly returns my every call, and the Archway staff who has used their expertise to publish my book.

All my sincere thanks to all of you!
Cima Balser